D1737255

Iraq in Transition

Other Titles Published by Westview Press in Cooperation with The Center for Strategic and International Studies Georgetown University

NATO: The Next Generation, edited by Robert E. Hunter

National Security and Strategic Minerals: An Analysis of U.S. Dependence on Foreign Sources of Cobalt, Barry M. Blechman

†*International Security Yearbook, 1984/85,* edited by Barry M. Blechman and Edward N. Luttwak

Bioenergy and Economic Development: Planning for Biomass Energy Programs in the Third World, William Ramsay

The Cuban Revolution: 25 Years Later, Hugh S. Thomas, Georges A. Fauriol, and Juan Carlos Weiss

The U.S. and the World Economy: Policy Alternatives for New Realities, edited by John Yochelson, with a foreword by William Brock

The Emerging Pacific Community: A Regional Perspective, edited by Robert L. Downen and Bruce Dickson

Modern Weapons and Third World Powers, Rodney W. Jones and Steven A. Hildreth

Under Pressure: U.S. Industry and the Challenges of Structural Adjustment, edited by Catherine Stirling and John Yochelson

Forecasting U.S. Electricity Demand: Trends and Methodologies, edited by Adela Maria Bolet

Political and Economic Trends in the Middle East: Implications for U.S. Policy, edited by Shireen Hunter

†Available in hardcover and paperback.

About the Book and Editor

After twenty-five years of thinly veiled hostility, U.S. relations with post-monarchial Iraq have warmed dramatically. Simultaneously, Iraq's sovereignty has become the keystone of Gulf stability, due to Iraq's military and economic resilience and to the rise of Khomeini's Iran and the waning of Saudi influence. In this book, five leading analysts explore the maturing Iraqi revolution, Iraq's long-term role in the Gulf, and the factors that will affect the future of U.S.-Iraqi political and commercial relations. The authors argue that continuing U.S. interest in the Middle East will demand changes in the U.S. approach toward Iraq. Future cooperation between the two countries, they believe, must be based on increased understanding by the United States of Iraq's people and leaders, and, most important, Iraqi response to the burden of a continuing war.

Frederick W. Axelgard is a Fellow in Middle East Studies at the Center for Strategic and International Studies, Georgetown University.

Published in Cooperation with
the Center for Strategic and International Studies
Georgetown University

Iraq in Transition

A Political, Economic, and Strategic Perspective

edited by Frederick W. Axelgard

Foreword by Robert G. Neumann

Westview Press / Boulder, Colorado

Mansell Publishing / London, England

This book is included in Westview's Special Studies on the Middle East.

Copyright © 1986 by The Center for Strategic and International Studies

Published in 1986 in the United States of America by Westview Press, Inc.; Frederick A. Praeger, Publisher; 5500 Central Avenue, Boulder, Colorado 80301

Published in 1986 in Great Britain by Mansell Publishing Limited, 6 All Saints Street, London N1 9RL, England

Library of Congress Cataloging-in-Publication Data
Main entry under title:
Iraq in transition.
   (Westview special studies on the Middle East)
   Includes index.
   Contents: Introduction / by Frederick Axelgard—
Iraq's domestic politics / by Adeed Dawisha—The
Iraqi economy / by Jonathan Crusoe—[etc.]
   1. Iraq—Politics and government—Addresses, essays,
lectures. I. Axelgard, Frederick W. II. Series.
DS79.65.I724 1986   320.9567   85-31525
ISBN 0-8133-0352-4

British Library Cataloguing-in-Publication Data
Iraq in transition : a political, economic
   and strategic perspective.
   1. Iraq—Economic conditions 2. Iraq
   —Politics and government 3. Iraq—
History—1958-
I. Axelgard, Frederick W.
330.9567'043   DS79.65
ISBN 0-7201-1821-2

This book was produced without formal editing by the publishers.

Printed and bound in the United States of America

10   9   8   7   6   5   4   3   2   1

Contents

Foreword

One of the main objectives of the Center for Strategic and International Studies of Georgetown University is to provide clear analyses of emergent international developments and their implications for U.S. interests. The Middle East Studies Program of CSIS therefore takes pride in the publication of this volume, *Iraq in Transition*. It treats a country whose potential economic and political significance has long been recognized as vast, but whose domestic instability and international unpredictability have helped discourage substantial interaction with the United States. Now, out of the fog of the Iran-Iraq war, new alignments in Iraq's domestic, regional, and international politics have paved the way for a reassessment of former views.

The changes that have occurred during the last twenty-five years in U.S. relations with Iraq are indeed startling in many respects. Before 1958, Iraq was the Arab country closest to the United States and the backbone of the now-defunct Baghdad Pact. But on July 14, 1958, this abruptly changed when the government of Nuri Said was overthrown in a bloody coup. Thereafter, relations between the two countries deteriorated quickly, from warm to tense to nonexistent.

A period of intense political instability approached its end when the Arab Ba'th (Renaissance) Socialist Party seized power in 1968, although real stability was firmly established only in 1979 when Saddam Hussein became president. With clear foresight, King Hassan II of Morocco told me in 1975, while I served as U.S. ambassador to that country, that Saddam Hussein—who had already emerged as Iraq's strongman—was fundamentally different from his predecessors and that the United States should see in this the harbinger of closer relations. And it is Saddam Hussein who has gradually moved Iraq towards more cordial relations with the United States. Diplomatic relations between the two countries, broken since 1967, were formally restored in 1984, but prior to that date a U.S. Interest Section in Baghdad and its Iraqi equivalent in Washington helped smooth the path, and economic relations became quite significant.

In addition to being the fourth largest Arab country in population, Iraq under the Ba'th Party has developed as a center of Arab nationalism and secularism, which places it in direct confrontation with the resurgent tide of Islamic fundamentalism. The United States as well as the moderate Arab regimes see in this upsurge a danger to the whole area's relations with the West. Hence Washington concluded some time ago that an Iranian victory over Iraq would be detrimental to the United States. The Soviet Union has come to somewhat similar conclusions. All this has created a growing interest in establishing even closer ties between the United States and Iraq, in both the political and economic realms. U.S. business interest in Iraq's market and investment opportunity has also steadily increased and should accelerate after the long war between Iraq and Iran has come to an end.

Iraq and Iraqi-U.S. relations have been the topic of a number of activities organized by the CSIS Middle East Program in the recent past. Generous and consistent financial support for these activities has been contributed by a number of corporations and foundations, and their assistance is gratefully acknowledged. Their interest collectively—and correctly—underscores the significance of the many opportunities that the future holds should U.S.-Iraqi relations stabilize on their present upward course.

Robert G. Neumann, Director
CSIS Middle East Studies
Former U.S. Ambassador

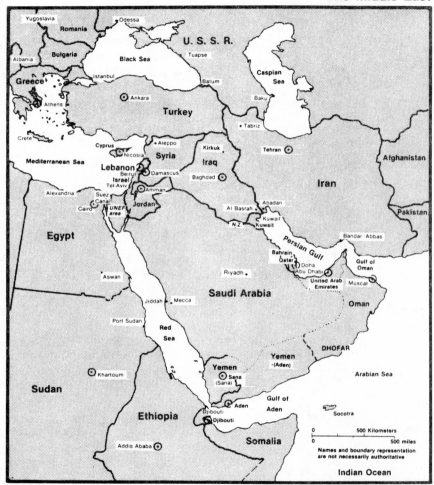

The Middle East

Source: U.S. Department of State.

1

War and Oil: Implications for Iraq's Postwar Role in Gulf Security

Frederick W. Axelgard

Iraq in Transition is an attempt to present insights into Iraq's response—in political, economic, and foreign policy terms—to the trauma of its ongoing war with Iran. Its main justification is neither the war nor the apparent evolution in Iraq's political and economic outlook. Rather its justification is Iraq's unchanging status as a major regional power and the belief that continuing U.S. interest in the Middle East, particularly in the Persian/Arab Gulf, in coming years will require more serious consideration of Iraq's role in the U.S. approach to the region. Although the precise nature of this role is yet to be determined, it will almost certainly include moving U.S.-Iraqi interaction toward a more open dialogue, and possibly discussion of limited U.S.-Iraqi cooperation to maintain a strategic balance in the Gulf between Iran, Saudi Arabia, and Iraq itself.

A growing dialogue with Iraq must be founded on an expanding understanding of the country, its leaders, and their response to the burden of the war. Consequently, the Middle East Program of the Georgetown University Center for Strategic and International Studies invited four distinguished scholars and analysts to address a seminar on the topic of "Iraq: Political, Economic, and Strategic Perspectives of a Country in Transition," which was held in May of 1985. At that seminar Jonathan Crusoe, Adeed Dawisha, Edmund Ghareeb, and Mark Katz presented the papers that are published here to contribute to the understanding needed for constructive U.S. policy choices vis-à-vis Iraq.

Although the United States did not have an independent policy toward Iraq until well into the 1950s (in deference to the prevalent British influence in the country), U.S. decision makers were conscious of Iraq's significance for regional policy early in the postwar era. In 1946, the State Department concluded,

> It will be increasingly necessary for us to maintain closer relations with Iraq, since our standing in the entire area will to a considerable degree be dependent on the attitude of Iraq toward the United States.[1]

But U.S. efforts to ground a portion of its regional strategy in Iraq, following the collapse of British prestige at Suez, were cut short by the 1958 revolution in Baghdad. The advent of revolutionary rule in Iraq inaugurated a prolonged period of tension with the United States, and mutual understanding dimmed even further when Baghdad severed its diplomatic relations with the United States during the 1967 war. Thus, throughout the 1960s and 1970s Iraq was considered beyond the pale of constructive involvement in any bilateral or regional aspect of U.S. Middle East policy. Not until the 1981 visit to Baghdad of then-Deputy Assistant Secretary of State Morris Draper, who was promoting the strategic consensus policy of Secretary of State Haig, was there a serious indication that Iraq might have a place in the thinking of U.S. policymakers regarding regional stability.

From 1981 to 1984 the scope and frequency of interaction between Baghdad and Washington expanded quickly, mostly because of the common threat posed to U.S. and Iraqi interests by the Iranian revolution. This rapprochement was formalized in November 1984 by the restoration of full diplomatic relations between the United States and Iraq. Since that time, other practical steps toward improving commercial relations and upgrading technological exchange have been taken, including the drafting of a general U.S.-Iraqi trade agreement and approval for the sale of advanced computer technology.

The time is ripe, therefore, to step back and examine the major factors determining Iraq's regional and international standing, particularly as they might affect the country's role in the future stability of the Gulf. In this essay a context will be set for the ensuing discussions of Iraq's domestic political and economic framework and key elements of its foreign policy, by focusing on two fundamental realities that affect all aspects of Iraqi national life. The first reality, the war with Iran, has probably become the most important single event in Iraq's modern history, not only because of the devastating loss of life and the billions of dollars in damages, but also because new contours in its domestic and international affairs have been forged. The second reality is Iraq's determined effort to expand its oil exports and reinstate the country as a major petroleum exporter within the next two or three years, whether the war with Iran ends or not.

The Gulf War

After five years, the Iran-Iraq war remains a stalemate because neither party is capable of imposing its will by military means, and Iran explicitly rejects a negotiated approach to resolving the dispute. If Iran's demand for the removal of Iraqi President Saddam Hussein and the Iraqi Ba'th Party persists, activity on all the war fronts—the tanker war in the Gulf, the ground war along the entire 1,200 kilometer border, the raids on nonmilitary targets in the cities, and international diplomacy—will continue unabated, but with little chance of eroding the underlying standoff in the foreseeable future.

The Oil War

After years of suspense over the war's potential impact on oil traffic, the tanker war in the Gulf began in earnest in March 1984. The confirmed toll in damages to shipping climbed quickly, although less quickly than Iraqi claims. According to a study published by *Lloyd's List* in March 1985, 55 oil tankers had been attacked in the Gulf since May 1981, 49 of them since late March 1984. The report also indicated that Iraq (which had been reponsible for almost two-thirds of such attacks) had shifted its focus from strikes in the northernmost sector of the Gulf to attacks further south, nearer the Iranian ports at Kharg Island and Bushehr.[2]

This modification in strategy suggested some of the difficulty Iraq had in damaging Iran's war machine by sharply reducing its oil exports. Notwithstanding Iraq's attacks, Iran produced an average of nearly 2.2 million barrels per day (b/d) of oil in 1984, while exports of 1.7 million b/d resulted in revenues of almost $17 billion.[3] Although this constituted a 23 percent reduction in revenues from 1983, part of this decline was due to market forces rather than Iraqi attacks, and the resultant impact on Iran's war effort in 1984 was negligible in any case.

January 1985 was the first month in which Iran's oil output dropped dramatically, to 1.4 million b/d, apparently as a result of intensive Iraqi bombing throughout the month of December. Iran's response was to begin shuttling oil on its own or Iranian-chartered tankers from Kharg to Sirri Island, an off-loading point lower in the Gulf, thus reducing the exposure of commercial tankers in the northern Gulf war zone. Iranian production and export levels rebounded immediately in February 1985, a setback for Iraq which certainly spurred its decision to escalate its air attacks against on-shore civilian targets in March.

The tanker war that began in early 1984 was preceded by an international crisis of nerves caused by France's sale of sophisticated aircraft and missiles to Iraq in late 1983. This sale, and the exchange of threats against Gulf shipping and the Strait of Hormuz that attended it, visibly increased the level of U.S. concern about the conflict. The Reagan administration reportedly sought to discourage the French sale and simultaneously asserted its intent to maintain unhindered passage through the Strait of Hormuz. In addition, when Iran responded to Iraq's attacks by hitting ships using Kuwaiti and Saudi ports, U.S. President Ronald Reagan outspokenly criticized Iran's attacks on the ships of "neutral nations" and expressed understanding for Iraq's attacks as an effort to undermine Iranian commerce.[4] Nevertheless, neither Iran's attacks on neutral shipping nor the Saudi air force's shooting down of invading Iranian aircraft in June 1984 changed Washington's underlying attitude that the threat posed by the tanker war was "not unmanageable".[5]

In August 1985, however, Iraq launched its first sustained and (apparently) effective series of attacks on Iran's main export terminal at Kharg Island. Extensive damage was reportedly inflicted on the loading jetties on either side of the island and on pumping and storage facilities on Kharg itself. Weeks after the attacks began, however, there were still seriously contradictory reports as to how much oil Iran was able to export: estimates varied from 100–200 thousand b/d to 1.2 million b/d.[6] Nevertheless, Iraq's success in penetrating Kharg's defenses loomed as a potential turning point in the war, in technical if not yet political terms. Thus, as the war entered its sixth year, the Gulf sector remained its major flashpoint and the arena most capable of changing the overall course of the conflict.

The Onshore War

In comparison with the exchange of attacks on oil targets, the recent ground war between Iran and Iraq has been far more bloody and less creative. Following Iran's human wave offensives in February 1984, Iraq waited for months for what Tehran announced would be its "final offensive." It never came. Minor skirmishes in the northern border areas at the end of the year provided a distraction from the protracted face-off between scores of thousands of troops in the southern sector, but only served to emphasize the absence of sustained advances anywhere on the ground.

Iraq appeared to anticipate another major Iranian buildup when it carried out small-scale offensive maneuvers against the Iranian lines at the end of January 1985. These operations seemed designed to keep Iran's strategic planners offguard by reminding them that Iraq retained a ground-offensive capability even if it had not been used in over two years. Just weeks later, after Iran successfully evaded Iraq's "blockade" of Kharg Island with the help of its shuttle service to Sirri Island, and after a United Nations study criticized Iraq and Iran equally for mistreatment of prisoners of war, Iraq's restraint disappeared. It began a large-scale aerial bombing campaign which focussed on industrial targets in important Iranian cities. Iran quickly retaliated with bombings and artillery barrages against Iraqi cities. This cycle dissolved a U.N.-sponsored cease-fire against civilian targets that had been concluded in June 1984.

The reasons for Iraq's aggressiveness were several. First was the need to disrupt a suspected Iranian military buildup. In addition, new tactics were in order once it became clear that the flow of Iran's oil had not been seriously curtailed by the tanker war. Third, and perhaps most fundamental, was Iraq's clear disappointment over the continued failure of international pressure to affect Iranian intransigence in any way. Thus Baghdad adopted what was termed "a defensive offense," and yet another phase in the war began.[7]

The significance of this new development was temporarily overshadowed by Iran's launching of yet another offensive in southern Iraq. In a week-long battle (March 12–18), which saw some of the heaviest ground fighting of the war thus far, Iran is believed to have sent over 100 thousand troops through the Hawizah marshes, where for the first time they penetrated to the Tigris River and temporarily seized a portion of the strategic Baghdad-Basrah highway. Iran's logistical inability to back up these penetrations quickly negated their immediate military significance, and Iraqi counterattacks succeeded in pushing the Iranian forces back into the marshes, although reportedly not back to their original starting point.

Casualties throughout the course of the war have been notoriously difficult to estimate, and the spring 1985 operations were no exception. U.S. officials were quoted as approximating "tens of thousands" of Iranian casualties,[8] while other independent estimates suggested casualties of 20 thousand for Iran and 10 thousand for Iraq.[9] Nor is it precisely clear what kind of forces the Iranians used in this fighting. Some reports suggested that regular military troops combined with volunteers played a larger part in planning and implementing this year's offensive than had been the case in 1984.[10] Other reports, however, stressed that Iranian tactics in 1985 had changed little, if at all, from 1984, recalling the image of human waves of untrained, often unarmed, and thoroughly unprepared Iranian men and boys rushing headlong into well-orchestrated Iraqi defenses.[11]

Introducing a disturbing new facet to its mode of assault, Iran and/or its supporters inside Iraq carried out four or five bombing attacks on Baghdad while the penetration across the Hawizah marshes was being executed. The origin of these (and subsequent) bombings was shrouded for a time with mystery. The official Iraqi explanation, issued by Saddam Hussein several days after the bombings began, was that Iran had fired long-range surface-to-surface missiles—apparently obtained from Libya or Syria—at Baghdad.[12] This explanation was generally accepted as valid, although several of the attacks in question (particularly the first one, which caused extensive damage to the upper levels of the central bank building) were attributed by Western diplomats to locally detonated explosions.[13] This suggested the possibility of a renewed terror campaign by the Shi'ite al-Da'wa, an underground extremist organization allied with Iran, which had not operated effectively in Baghdad since the end of 1982. Like its ground offensive, however, Iran's dozen or so strikes on Baghdad failed to produce any telling military or political impact on Iraq.

Iraq's attacks on Iranian cities, particularly Tehran, were different, however. Even as the ground war was raging, Iraq carried out intensive air strikes on cities across the countryside of Western Iran and announced a blockade that cut sharply into the commercial air traffic entering Iran.[14] There then followed an air siege of Iran in which Iraqi jets carried out sustained nightly bombing raids that precipitated the flight of thousands of Tehran's citizens to the suburbs. This siege was the most forceful element of Iraq's new policy of "total peace or total war," which rejected partial truces such as a cease-fire on civilian targets, and demanded that Iran agree to comprehensive negotiations before Baghdad would alter its aggressive posture.

This new Iraqi policy appears to have had some impact on Iran, although less than Iraq desired. Antiwar demonstrations occurred in Tehran, not only among the middle classes of the northern suburbs, which have for some time been known to oppose continuation of the war, but also in the poorer suburbs of southern Tehran, where support for the Khomeini regime has been strongest.[15] Opposition to the war inside Iran subsequently went public in the statements of Mehdi Bazargan, the first prime minister of Iran's Islamic republic and leader of the small Liberation Party, the only opposition political movement allowed to exist above ground in Iran. Bazargan's criticism of Iran's policy in the war took on sharper political meaning when it became part of his platform as a potential candidate in the Iranian presidential election scheduled for August 1985.[16] Bazargan's subsequent disqualification from the election was interpreted in part to mean that his antiwar views were too volatile to be allowed a full airing inside Iran.

These and other developments suggest a tentative two-fold conclusion about the development of Iranian attitude about the ground war through 1985. First, popular anti-war sentiment appeared to reach its highest point in the war thus far. A potentially significant change in tactics—Khomeini's call in June 1985 for a "defensive jihad," presumably a shift to smaller-scale, non-frontal attacks—appears to have been caused by such political pressures.[17] The second point to be made, however, is that these pressures had not become strong enough to alter the regime's fundamental strategy of continuing to fight until the Ba'thist government in Baghdad is deposed.

Gulf War Diplomacy

Without a change in Iran's underlying strategy, regional and international diplomacy has remained a key focus of activity with regard to the Gulf war. Some recent hope must be taken from Iran and Iraq's adherence to the June 1984 UN-sponsored cease-fire on attacks against civilian targets, and their allowance of a UN study of the two sides' treatment of prisoners of war.

These efforts were part of a stream of diplomatic undertakings that has continued unabated since the war began in 1980. Over a score of such initiatives were launched in the first few months of 1985 alone, involving individual states with a strong interest in the conflict (such as Kuwait, Saudi Arabia, Egypt, Algeria, the United Arab Emirates, and Japan), the Gulf Cooperation Council (GCC), the Arab League, and leaders of the Nonaligned Movement and the Islamic Conference Organization.

The most striking diplomatic campaign, however, was undertaken by UN Secretary General Javier Perez de Cuellar. Mr. Perez de Cuellar made a highly publicized trip to the Gulf in April 1985, immediately after the conclusion of Iran's spring offensive, to seek a basis on which to negotiate a reduction in tension between the two sides. Hopes for his success were stimulated by the fact that the UN General Assembly and its leader are held in credible esteem by both Iran and Iraq,[18] although Iran strongly rejects the UN Security Council. From all visible indications, however, de Cuellar's visits to Tehran and Baghdad had no lasting effect. Iran's leadership refused to consider broad-based negotiations for an overall settlement of the war, but was ready to discuss a limited truce in civilian areas. Iraq, on the other hand, insisted that it would agree only to discuss a comprehensive cessation of hostilities. Nevertheless Secretary General de Cuellar later stated that his visit had improved the prospects of a settlement of the war, a conclusion he may have reached in part because of a lull in attacks on civilian targets, which began at the time of his mediation effort.

Attention has also focused on recent Iranian diplomacy, which has aimed to reduce Iran's isolation, both regionally and internationally. A striking element of this pattern was the surprise visit of Saudi Arabia's Foreign Minister Saud al-Faisal to Iran in May 1985, the first official visit of a Saudi minister to Tehran since Khomeini came to power.[19] The limited accounts of what Prince Saud discussed with Iranian officials indicate only that he was told Iran intends to continue the war with Iraq. Observers agreed that the major significance of the exchange was Iran's resumption of public ties with Iraq's major supporter among the Gulf countries. In addition, Iran followed this contact up with a concentrated diplomatic campaign to reassure the other Arab states of the Gulf of its benign intentions in the region, and particularly to affirm that Iran had played no role in the attempted assassination of the Amir of Kuwait in late May.[20]

Notwithstanding these and other evidences of Iran's increasing interest in regional and international diplomacy, it remains clear that there has been no fundamental shift in Iran's commitment to continue the war.

The Oil Outlook

The immediate stimulus behind Baghdad's intensive oil export expansion program was a financial crisis, with threatening political implications, that came to a head in late 1982 and early 1983. Iraq possessed an estimated $35 billion in foreign reserves when its war with Iran began in September 1980, and these disappeared quickly as Saddam Hussein combined his costly economic development programs in 1980–1982 with military expenditures of $1–2 billion per month. Replenishment of Iraq's financial resources was impossiible, as Iraqi oil exports had dropped drastically at the beginning of the war and were reduced another 50 percent in April 1982 when Syria cut off all Iraqi exports across its territory (see table 1). Finally, the loss in 1982 of most of the direct subventions Iraq had been receiving from its Arab supporters in the Gulf added to the burden, placing Iraq in a desperate economic and political position from which many observers felt it might not recover.

TABLE 1. Iraqi Oil Production during the Iran-Iraq War
(In Thousands of Barrels per Day)

	1980	1981	1982	1983	1984	1985
January		400	1,300	850	1,150	1,250
February		700	1,400	850	1,000	1,250
March		960	1,200	900	1,200	1,200
April		800	800	950	1,200	1,370
May		900	800	1,000	1,200	1,300
June		1,000	800	1,000	1,225	1,370
July		900	800	1,050	1,200	1,450
August	[3,400]	800	800	1,100	1,250	1,400
September	2,900	1,000	800	1,050	1,300	
October	150	1,000	800	1,100	1,200	
November	300	1,100	800	1,150	1,250	
December	550	1,200	800	1,050	1,250	
Average Daily Production	2,646.4	897.4	922.5	1,077	1,203	
Annual Revenue* ($ billion)	26.0	10.4	9.5	8.4	10.4	

Source: Petroleum Intelligence Weekly.
*Estimated. *Petroleum Economist*, July 1985.

Iraq's Response to Economic Crisis

But the Ba'th leadership in Baghdad moved aggressively to defuse its cash-flow crisis. Its first achievement was to obtain postponement of payments owed to foreign contractors who had become involved in the massive economic expansion of the prior two years. At the same time, Iraqi leaders laid the basis for a longer-term solution to the country's economic insecurity by beginning an aggressive program to improve its oil export position. The decision was taken to expand the flow of oil through Iraq's only operating export channel, a pipeline across Turkey to the Mediterranean port of Ceyhan, using anti-drag chemicals. Exports were thereby increased to 700 thousand barrels per day (b/d) by mid-1983.[21] Also at about this time, Saudi Arabia and Kuwait began to export an estimated 300 thousand b/d for Iraq's account under a time exchange agreement. This oil, taken primarily from the Saudi-Kuwaiti neutral zone but apparently assigned to no country's OPEC production quota, has provided Iraq with an indispensable $3 billion in added annual revenues.[22]

It was also decided to expand the trans-Turkey pipeline's structural capacity (by looping the line and building additional pumping stations) to the level of 1 million b/d. A $120 million Euroloan for this project was secured in early 1983, and by the end of the summer of 1984, the desired expansion of capacity was achieved.[23] It is important to note that Iraq's strategic dependence on this pipeline since 1982 and the decision to expand it have contributed significantly to the evolution of a solid political, security, and economic relationship between Iraq and Turkey. Concern for the security of the pipeline, which has been sabotaged a number of times since the beginning of the war, (presumably by Kurdish elements) figured significantly in Baghdad's decision to allow two major incursions, in 1983 and 1984, by Turkish troops who pursued Kurdish insurgents into Iraqi territory.

The vulnerability of the Ceyhan pipeline, and the need to use more of Iraq's estimated 4 million b/d oil production capacity for exports, led it to pursue other pipeline options as well. During 1983 Iraqi officials conducted discussions with Saudi Arabia on the possible construction of an export line across Saudi territory, a concept which had been discussed since 1981 but never implemented. Most observers expected that Iraq's growing military strength, the strong ideological differences between the Iraqi and Saudi regimes, and the Saudis' desire not to provoke Islamic Iran by excessive support of Iraq, would preclude Saudi approval of the project. Thus many were surprised that an agreement was reached in late 1983 to build a system whose initial phase would be a 650 kilometer linkup from Iraq's southern oil fields to the trans-Saudi Arabia Petroline.[24] The contract to construct phase one was let in September 1984, and Iraq was expected to be able to export 500 thousand b/d of oil through this pipeline by the end of 1985.

Even as plans for Iraq's tie-in with the Saudi east-west line moved toward realization, Iraqi officials pursued discussion of at least three other options: a pipeline from central Iraq to the Jordanian port of Aqaba, an additional pipeline across Turkey, and a phase two of the Saudi project involving an independent Iraqi pipeline to the Red Sea. The Aqaba proposal, involving projected costs of around $1 billion and a capacity to export 1 million b/d of Iraqi oil, attracted wide attention both because of its scope and because of the potential for U.S. involvement. Diplomats indicate privately that the possibility of U.S. support for the pipeline surfaced in December 1983, during a visit to Baghdad by U.S. presidential envoy Donald Rumsfeld. In the ensuing months, momentum behind the Aqaba proposal grew and, for a brief time, even appeared to surpass that of the Saudi phase one project. Discussions broke down, however, over Iraq's insistence that any repayment obligations on the part of itself or Jordan should lapse if, and for as long as, Israel interfered with the pipeline's construction or operation. This impasse was not broken even by the U.S. Export-Import Bank's preliminary approval of nearly $500 million in credit guarantees to support Bechtel's participation in the project.[25] Since that time, Jordan has adopted an advocate's position and has undertaken periodic efforts to rekindle support for the pipeline.[26] Reportedly, consideration has even been given to an additional pipeline to carry the Iraqi oil across Sinai to Egypt's Sumed pipeline.[27] Nevertheless, current opinion holds that the Aqaba line has gone by the boards. Progress on other projects has reduced the need for such an undertaking, which has such intrinsic disadvantages as physical vulnerability, large expense, and potential political controversy.

As difficulties arose with the Aqaba proposal, attention shifted to the possibility of a second Iraqi oil export pipeline across Turkey. Turkey and Iraq reached agreement on the project in August 1984, in which a new pipeline would be built parallel to (and using the pumping stations of) the existing line. The overall addition to capacity is expected to be 500–600 thousand b/d at a cost of $550 million. Contracts for construction were signed in late summer of 1985, with pipeline completion by the end of 1986 or early 1987.

The largest and most expensive of Iraq's current export-expansion options is phase two of its Saudi project. Even following approval and the commencement of construction on phase one (the tie-in to Petroline), doubt surrounded the prospects for phase two. It was seen to possess all of the liabilities (for the Saudis) of phase one multiplied by a factor of more than two. Plans call for building an Iraqi pipeline to the Red Sea, which would permit 1.6 million b/d of oil exports (a net addition of 1.1 million b/d above and beyond phase one) and include nearly 1,000 kilometers of pipeline, a dozen new pumping stations, extensive loading and storage facilities at the Red Sea terminus as well as telecommunications and telecontrol systems—all for approximately $2 billion.[28] Such an expense at a time of budgetary cutbacks in Baghdad and weakening oil prices also reduced the probability that the project would be developed.

Notwithstanding these constraints, it became apparent in discussions held in Baghdad and Riyadh during the first months of 1985 that both Iraq and Saudi Arabia intended to move ahead with phase two. In May it was announced that Saudi officials had approved the route of the pipeline and the site for its terminus on the Red Sea, 50 kilometers south of Yanbu.[29] Tenders for construction were due to be let in late 1985, and completion of the entire system was expected by late 1987 or early 1988.

Iraq's Shut-In Oil Capacity

Before considering the cumulative picture presented by Iraq's on-going export-enhancement program, we will look briefly at Iraq's remaining export potential, which consists of those facilities that have been rendered inoperable by the Iran-Iraq war and by Syrian policies against Iraq.

When Syria shut off the old Iraq Petroleum Company (IPC) pipeline in 1982, some 400 thousand b/d of Iraqi oil was being channeled through it. This was not the first time, however, that Syria had interrupted Iraqi oil exports, and it may well not be the last, notwithstanding a statement by Iraq's First Deputy Prime Minister Taha Yassin Ramadan that the Syrian pipeline is "abandoned, because we will not need it after the opening of the new oil outlets through Saudi Arabia and Turkey."[30] Because it was closed by a political decision and not physical destruction, the IPC line is theoretically the easiest of Iraq's non-functioning oil export channels to reactivate. But the strong animus between Saddam Hussein and Syrian President Hafiz al-Assad that prompted the pipeline closure has not abated. Furthermore, numerous attempts by mediators enjoying good relations with both countries (e.g., the Soviet Union) to persuade Syria to reopen the line have proven unsuccessful.[31]

On the other hand, the rationale for Syria's cutoff of the IPC line only grows weaker with the passage of time. It was originally carried out at a time of monumental crisis as Iraq retreated from Iranian counterattacks, seemingly a propitious moment for Syria to take a ruthless, unbrotherly swipe at the rival Ba'thists in Baghdad. But Saddam Hussein has weathered the storm and appears less likely than ever to succumb to Iranian pressure. Syria's relationship with Iran, meanwhile, has lost much of its original luster, and with Iraq likely to achieve 2 million b/d in export capacity by 1987, the leverage inherent in the IPC line could disappear altogether. As completion of Iraq's new outlets across Saudi Arabia and Turkey draws near, Syria may well be forced to decide whether it can afford to lose permanently the transit fees and oil it once received because of this pipeline. Moreover, Syria's dependence on Saudi subsidies and Soviet military support shows no sign of abating, and both these powers are extremely interested in Syria reopening the pipeline for Iraq.

Iraq's other dormant oil export options are more conclusively inaccessible because of physical destruction and the undiminished intensity of the war with Iran. Prior to the war, Iraq had the capacity to export 4.5 million b/d from Mina al-Bakr and Khor al-Amaya, two offshore terminals located just outside the mouth of the disputed

TABLE 2. Growth of Iraq's Oil Export Pipeline System

Pipeline	Pipeline Capacity (million b/d)	Date of Pipeline Availability	Cumulative Export Capacity (million b/d)
Ceyhan	1.0	Summer 1984	1.0
Saudi Phase I	0.5	End of 1985	1.5
Ceyhan II	0.5–0.6	Early- to mid-1987	2.0–2.1
Saudi Phase II	1.6*	Mid-1987 to mid-1988	3.1–3.2

Source: Middle East Economic Digest and *Middle East Economic Survey.*
*With Saudi Phase I already exporting 500 thousand b/d, Saudi Phase II would provide a net addition of 1.1 million b/d to Iraq's export capacity.

Shatt al-Arab waterway. These terminals and the onshore facilities that fed them were attacked in the early stages of the war. Although the extent of damages has never been publicly discussed by Iraqi officials, an internal U.S. government estimate made in 1981 was that $8-10 billion in damages had been inflicted on Iraq's southern oil production and export facilities. Although major uncertainties about these facilities remain, observers agree that it would take 6-8 months after the end of hostilities before Iraq could resume exports, and then only at a level of 1 million b/d, by using temporary single-point mooring buoys that would bypass the damaged terminals. It would be at least another 4-6 months before exports from the terminals themselves could resume at prewar levels.

Iraq's Cumulative Scenario and the Oil-Marketing Outlook

The overall estimate is that Iraq's oil export capacity will expand to 1.5 million b/d when the first phase of its trans-Saudi project starts up in late 1985. By the end of 1986 or early 1987, it will expand to 2.0 or 2.1 million b/d with the completion of the second pipeline to Ceyhan. Finally, under an optimistic construction scenario, the second phase of the Saudi system could be ready by late 1987 or the beginning of 1988. Thus, whether the Gulf war ends or not, Iraq could acquire the capacity to resume oil exports at roughly prewar levels of 3.1–3.2 million b/d by early 1988 (see table 2).

Long before then, however, the matter of how to market some or all of this oil will have to be addressed. In March 1983, Iraq accepted from OPEC a reduced oil production quota of 1.2 million b/d. At the time this figure exceeded Iraq's needs because available export capacity was only around 650 thousand b/d and domestic consumption was roughly 250–300 thousand b/d. By early 1985, even without the tie-in to Petroline, Iraqi production was believed to exceed (slightly) its OPEC quota: exports to Ceyhan averaged between 900 thousand and 1 million b/d, overland truck exports to Jordan and Turkey were estimated at 100 thousand b/d, and domestic consumption remained at 250–300 thousand b/d.

Raising Iraq's production quota, discussion of which has been put off since early 1984, becomes an issue upon completion of the linkup with Petroline. This project raises Iraq's output to 1.7–1.8 million b/d. Because of the prevailing soft market, a controversy began to brew in early 1985 over whether completion of the tie-in should result in discontinuation of the 300 thousand b/d of oil Kuwait and Saudi Arabia have been producing for Iraq. Iraq was clearly disinclined to accept a connection between completion of the tie-in and cessation of the Kuwaiti-Saudi oil grant. Rather, Iraq's view was that this supply of oil was linked to the closure of the IPC line and should not be stopped until Syria has reversed its 1982 decision and reopened this pipeline.[32] Saudi Arabia and Kuwait, on the other hand, stressed their expectation that Iraq would start to pay back the time-exchange oil once its new pipelines begin to be completed.[33] In addition, Iraq repeatedly announced its intention to pursue a higher OPEC production quota when its new pipeline came onstream, a move that the rest of OPEC appeared determined to put off as long as possible.

Notwithstanding that events appeared to be coming to a head—completion of Iraq's pipeline spur, a major OPEC meeting to consider Iraq's production quota, and renewal of the Saudi-Kuwaiti agreement to supply oil for Iraq were all scheduled for the end of 1985 or early 1986—it is unlikely that a major confrontation will develop over this initial expansion of Iraqi output. A more probable scenario would be a tacit compromise whereby there is a reduction in the amount of Saudi and Kuwaiti oil supplied for Iraq, utilization of the new Iraqi pipeline at less than its full 500 thousand b/d capacity, Iraq's disposal of some portion of its new oil exports under barter (or near-barter) arrangements, and perhaps a marginal increase in Iraq's production quota to 1.5–1.8 million b/d.

The situation that will occur when the second pipeline to Ceyhan, Turkey is finished should also prove manageable. OPEC will then have to deal with pressures to increase Iraq's production quota to

2.2–2.3 million b/d. The oil market is not expected to harden sufficiently to create room for this oil through increased demand, and several other OPEC members (e.g., Nigeria and Venezuela) are ready to contest Iraq for increased production quotas. Nevertheless, several factors will not allow this situation to deteriorate to the point of seriously disrupting the oil market and the interests of Iraq and OPEC. First and foremost, all parties stand to suffer significantly from any precipitous action that would undermine the fragile oil market. Moreover, historically Iraq has strongly supported a united OPEC pricing and production mechanism and is sensitive to its present vulnerability. In this vein, Iraqi President Saddam Hussein recently declared that Iraq's capacity to export oil would return to prewar levels "in the near future, God willing." He then added, making a significant distinction between capacity and actual exports, "We will be able to export *all that the current circumstances in the world oil market allow for.*"[34]

The resolution of this dilemma will also be affected by the nature of Iraq's relations within OPEC, particularly with the Arab states of the Gulf, and the degree to which domestic economic and political circumstances might dictate the level of need for greater oil revenues. As the various chapters in this volume will show, Iraq's domestic and regional outlooks are not desperate. Although suspicions linger in the Gulf about Iraq's possible hegemonic ambitions in the area, Baghdad is, generally speaking, on better terms with these countries than perhaps at any time in the past 30 years. The legacy of the Gulf war has developed a sense of interdependence between Iraq and the Gulf states which, despite its negative premise, seems destined to continue and to expand rather than diminish. Here again, mutual self-interests imply probable conciliation and cooperation.

Domestically, the Iraqi regime appears to have stabilized its economic and political situation considerably since 1982–1983. The threat of internal subversion by Iraqi Shi'ites and Kurds has not materialized but has dissipated since the war turned into a defense of Iraqi soil, and a strengthened sense of Iraqi nationalism has emerged.[35] The economy, meanwhile, has held firm. Budgetary cutbacks have been absorbed, and with the continued patience of foreign creditors and gradual growth in oil export earnings, no major crises loom on the horizon. In fact, the Iraqi regime might well have sufficient means to widen its basis for domestic stability in the next few years if its oil production stabilizes in the range of 1.8–2.0 million b/d. Furthermore, should Iraq agree to maintain production at these levels— 35 to 50 percent below its prewar output—this might well provide sufficient long-term assurance to induce Saudi Arabia and the rest of OPEC to make the short-term adjustments needed to allow Iraqi production to expand without drastically affecting the oil market.

Iraq and the Future
of Western Interests in the Gulf

As this essay has briefly discussed and as the succeeding chapters explain in detail, Iraq has stabilized its course after experiencing war-induced upheavals in almost every aspect of its national life. If one assumes (a) that Iraq will survive intact to the end of its conflict with Iran, and (b) that it will do so by continuing to rely on flexible diplomacy, diversified sources of military supply, and an economic buildup that involves extensive interdependent linkages to neighboring countries, it is important to consider what the impact of these experiences might be on Iraq's future role in the Gulf, particularly so far as Western interests are concerned.

To the degree that it is discussed at all, this question is susceptible to uncreative, almost reflexive treatment. The image of postwar Iraq conjured up by foreign policy analysts bears a remarkable resemblance to the image they held of Iraq in the 1970s: a country whose regional ambitions and revolutionary zealousness put it at odds with the conservative Arab states of the Gulf and with U.S. interests in the stability and security of the area. Hence, the salient assumption is that a battle-hardened and militarily enlarged Iraq will be inclined to assert military and political hegemony in the Gulf.

A less fatalistic consideration of the question ought to be set forth, however. First, in domestic terms, notwithstanding its strong authoritarian basis, Iraq's leadership would have great difficulty generating political support for any regional "adventurism" given the country's present level of war fatigue, and what it would be after additional years of fighting. Close observers of the country agree virtually unanimously that the Ba'th will be obliged by domestic pressures (if it is not the party's own genuine intention) to focus heavily on domestic social and economic programs once the war is over. Second, in regional terms, a cessation of the war would probably mean only a tacit agreement with Iran that the costs of the conflict had become prohibitive, rather than elimination of hostility. In this case, Iraq would have little latitude for taking a belligerent posture but would have to remain sensitive to the concerns of its Arab neighbors in the Gulf in order to preclude their aligning with Iran.

To take a positive rather than a negative view of these same circumstances, Iraq has learned during the course of the war the value of local allies and international supporters. It has depended on these for its very survival and will presumably learn this fundamental political lesson even more fully by the time the fighting ends. Moreover, Iraq's postwar economic lifelines—trade relations as well as the physical network of oil pipelines and other overland transit routes—will involve sustained interdependencies with its neighbors. Thus, while postwar Iraq will be a regional force to be reckoned with, prevailing internal and external circumstances could well incline Baghdad to commit itself to regional coexistence and even cooperation, rather than confrontation.

For the United States, the implications of such a fundamentally constructive postwar Iraqi posture in the Gulf are several. To begin with, U.S. policy in the interim could encourage this eventuality. This observation implies no major change in Washington's current policy of having correct and steadily improving political relations with Baghdad, providing no military hardware for use in the war with Iran, and broadening the basis for extensive commercial exchange. If this path of policy is adhered to, and particularly if commercial relations develop appreciably, then strong mutual advantages are to be gained. The United States would finally gain significant access to its last major Middle East market—and potentially the most lucrative Arab-world market of the next two decades—at a time when the U.S. foreign trade deficit is mounting alarmingly. Iraq would gain widening access to the U.S. technology that it has long coveted. The full flowering of this commercial relationship probably cannot occur until after the end of the Gulf war. Yet both the lucrative potential of the Iraqi market and the bilateral and regional political benefits of Iraq ascribing serious value to its relationship with the United States suggest that Washington would be well advised to encourage this relationship to develop quickly.

Such a growing, albeit limited relationship with Iraq could also figure importantly in long-term U.S. security policy toward the Gulf as a whole, for it could tend to reduce any inclination Iraq might have to destabilize the conservative Arab regimes of the Gulf. A broader political understanding with the United States, supplemented by a healthy flow of commodities and technology, would add to Iraq's local interdependencies as reasons to support the regional status quo. On the other hand, even after Khomeini passes from the scene, U.S. relations with Iran are likely to face inherent limitations. It would appear infeasible to expect Iran to once again be party to a policy such as the "twin pillars" doctrine. In the absence of such a predominant regional alignment, and assuming that it remains politically impossible for the United States to gain major, direct access to bases in other host countries in the Gulf,[36] then the best alternative would be for Washington to balance its relations among the major actors in the area—Iran, Saudi Arabia, and Iraq.

A basis for implementing this alternative—and gaining the potential, long-term advantages it could produce—is now taking shape as the formal U.S.-Iraqi relationship gets off the ground after almost 20 years of severed diplomatic relations. Admittedly, some thought must be given to the possibility that an overly close U.S.-Iraqi embrace would unnecessarily damage the prospects for an eventual resumption of civil relations between Iran and the United States. Nevertheless, Iraq's continued strong relations with the Soviet Union, the U.S. policy of not supplying arms to either party in the Gulf war, and self-evident political realities in both countries should prevent an intimate or strategic relationship from developing between Washington and Baghdad.

Notes

1. "Memorandum by Mr. Adrian B. Colquitt of the Division of Near Eastern Affairs, Secret [Washington, February 4, 1946]," in *Foreign Relations: 1946*, Vol. 7 (Washington, D.C.: Government Printing Office, 1969), pp. 568–569.

2. *Middle East Economic Survey (MEES)*, April 1, 1985.

3. *Petroleum Economist*, July 1985.

4. Frederick W. Axelgard, "The Tanker War in the Gulf," *Middle East Insight*, Vol. 3, No. 6 (November/December 1984): 29–30.

5. *Middle East International*, June 29, 1984.

6. See respectively, *Oil and Gas Journal*, October 14, 1985, and *MEES*, October 14, 1985.

7. Gerald F. Seib, "Iraq Takes Up Aggressive Posture in Iran War, Hoping to Force Opponent to Negotiating Table," *Wall Street Journal*, March 12, 1985.

8. *New York Times*, March 20, 1985.

9. *MEES*, March 25, 1985.

10. Ibid., and *Middle East International*, March 22, 1985.

11. *Washington Post*, March 25, 1985.

12. Ibid., March 29, 1985.

13. Author's interview with diplomatic sources in Baghdad.

14. Jim Muir, "Iraq Turns Up the Heat on Iran," *Christian Science Monitor*, March 22, 1985.

15. *London Observer*, May 5, 1984, p. 14. See also *The Economist*, May 4, 1985, pp. 38–39, and June 22, 1985, p. 35.

16. *Le Monde*, May 2, 1985, as found in Joint Publications Research Service (JPRS), *Near East/South Asia Report*, June 6, 1985, pp. 97–99; and *Christian Science Monitor*, June 11, 1985.

17. "New Phase in the Gulf War," *Khaleej Times*, June 25, 1985, cited in Foreign Broadcast Information Service (FBIS), *Daily Report: Middle East and Africa*, June 26, 1985, p. C4.

18. Gary Sick, "A Chance to End the Iran-Iraq War," *New York Times*, June 13, 1985.

19. This visit was preceded several months earlier by unconfirmed reports of high-level Saudi-Iranian contacts in Mecca, during the annual pilgrimage, and at the United Nations in New York. See *The Times* (London), September 15, 1984; and (clandestine) Radio Nejat-e Iran, September 27, 1984, cited in JPRS, *Near East/South Asia Report*, December 18, 1984, p. 130.

20. *MEES*, June 10, 1985.

21. American Embassy Baghdad, *Foreign Economic Trends and Their Implications for the United States: Iraq* (Washington, D.C.: U.S. Department of Commerce, June 1985), p. 8.

22. American Embassy Baghdad, *Foreign Economic Trends and Their Implications for the United States: Iraq* (Washington, D.C.: U.S. Department of Commerce, April 1984), p.7.

23. Notwithstanding this expansion in capacity, actual throughput of the Ceyhan line has not yet stabilized. Rather, it has vacillated above and below the 1 million b/d level. See *Petroleum Intelligence Weekly*, July 15, 1985.

24. *MEES*, November 28, 1983.

25. "Decisive Yet Cautious," *Middle East International*, June 29, 1984.

26. *MEES*, March 4, 1985.

27. Ibid., March 25, 1985.

28. *Middle East Economic Digest*, May 4, 1984.

29. *MEES*, May 20, 1985.

30. Ibid., June 17, 1985.

31. *Al-Majallah* (London), March 31–April 6, 1984, p. 3, as translated in JPRS, *Near East/South Asia Report*, May 21, 1984, p. 1.

32. *MEES*, July 15, 1985.

33. *Petroleum Intelligence Weekly*, July 22, 1985. This viewpoint was also expressed to the author in conversations held in Riyadh in February 1985.

34. Speech broadcast in Baghdad, July 16, 1985, as translated in FBIS, *Daily Report: Middle East and Africa*, July 17, 1985, p. E5. Emphasis added.

35. *The Economist*, October 20, 1984, pp. 15–16, refers to the "triumph of national feeling" within the Iraqi Shi'ite community in recent years.

36. Problems in U.S. politico-military relations with the Arab countries of the Gulf appear likely to continue or to grow rather than diminish. A fundamental reason for this difficulty—the disagreement these countries have with the nature of U.S. support for Israel—will probably not disappear in the foreseeable future. Indeed, it recently contributed to Saudi Arabia's dropping plans to purchase sophisticated aircraft and other weapons from the United States and concluding a multibillion dollar agreement with Great Britain instead.

Yet another complication for U.S. military policy in the Gulf arose in September 1985 when Oman, which has granted the United States a measure of access to military facilities near the Gulf, surprisingly announced the establishment of diplomatic relations with the Soviet Union. While this Omani gesture might have little practical impact in the immediate future, Washington has not accepted it as an encouraging sign.

2

The Politics of War:
Presidential Centrality,
Party Power, Political Opposition

Adeed Dawisha

Even with a debilitating war against Iran, Iraq has boasted a stable political system that has remained essentially unchanged since the Ba'thist takeover of power in July 1968. This is in marked contrast to the period, between 1958 and 1968, which witnessed four violent changes of power. The stability of the recent period is due primarily to the highly active Ba'th Party, guided by the single-minded and highly ambitious Saddam Hussein.

The Decision Making Elite

The National Action Charter, proclaimed by the late President Ahmad Hasan al-Bakr in November of 1971, defined the Iraqi political system as

> the legal expression for the interests and aspirations of the social classes and groups it represents. Since the Arab Ba'th Socialist Party represents the interests of the broadest masses from among workers, peasants and other hard toiling groups, the political system which the Party sought to build up . . . is as defined by the Seventh Regional Conference of the Party: a democratic, revolutionary and unitary system.[1]

The Ba'th party, therefore, supports Iraq's political system both politically and ideologically.

Ba'thist ideas began to penetrate the ideological orientations of Iraqi society after World War II, and by 1958, when the monarchy was overthrown, the Ba'th Party had established itself as a major political force in the country. By 1963, it had gained enough strength

21

to take control of the government, albeit only for a period of months before it was itself overthrown by non-Ba'thist nationalist officers. Its ideological appeal, and its underground activities, continued to grow until July 1968 when the party engineered a series of coups that established it as the core political organization in the country.

Michel Aflaq founded the Ba'th Party in the late 1930s and was its first secretary-general. Ba'th ideology, as formulated by Aflaq, rests on three basic principles: the unity and freedom of the Arab nation within its Arab homeland; a belief in the uniqueness of the Arab nation; and a belief in the special mission of the Arab people, aimed at the promotion of humanitarianism and the eradication of colonialism. For the party to succeed in achieving these aims, Aflaq insisted that the Ba'th movement had to be nationalist, populist, socialist, and revolutionary. Through this "revolutionary zeal," according to Aflaq, the most revered and fundamental of Ba'thist goals would be achieved— the organic political unity of all the Arabs.

Three years after taking power, the Iraqi Ba'thists tried to broaden their support base. Thus, at the end of 1971, the regime produced the National Action Charter, which seemed to loosen Ba'thist control of political power by opening the system to other "nationalist" and "progressive" forces. According to the charter, the Ba'th Party and the regime were opening "the way before all national forces to participate in deepening the revolutionary march-forward and con- solidating its foundation." This would make the country "a living and genuine model for mature revolutionary action in the Arab homeland and spring-board for the Arab revolution."[2] Three months later, two Communists and two pro-Egypt Arab nationalists entered the Iraqi Cabinet in an ostensible exercise of power sharing.

In reality, however, the Ba'th Party continued to be the central and authoritiative institutional organ, for even as the National Front was being formed, Iraq's President Bakr unequivocally asserted that "no party other than the Ba'th Party will be allowed to carry out any form of political or organizational activity within the armed forces."[3] And indeed the General Secretary of the Iraqi Communist Party (ICP) endorsed Ba'thist centrality in his speech to the Third Congress of the ICP held in Baghdad in 1976.

> The Ba'th Party is the leader of the revolution and the political authority of the state, and as such has a significant role in leading the National Front. The Communist Party endorses this position. It also approves the progressive and revolutionary achievements that are being accom- plished and considers them fundamental and advantageous steps on the road of building socialism in Iraq.[4]

It was thus clear to all parties that, notwithstanding the National Front, the Ba'th Party remained the sole governing party in Iraq.

In the personalized political world of the Arab Middle East, however, it is not so much the party itself, even one as prestigious as the Ba'th Party, but the key person within the party who tends to direct the country's political orientation. The Ba'th Party certainly has influence, for it sets limitations on the chief executive's freedom of maneuver. Yet power, including political and even, in certain cases, ideological direction, resides in the final analysis with the chief executive; for to set limitations is not to formulate or reverse policies and to argue a point is not to make the argument stick.

In analyzing governmental values and policies, therefore, the focus of attention ought to be directed toward the head of the party. After the Ba'th Party's assumption of power in 1968, the man who filled this central role was Saddam Hussein. First as assistant secretary-general of the party and vice president of the republic, and more authoritatively after July 1979, as president, secretary-general of the party, and commander in chief of the armed forces, Saddam Hussein dominated the decision-making process, determining the country's foreign policy orientations.

Hussein's centrality could be explained by a several factors. In the first place, he entrusted a number of sensitive positions within the political leadership to members of his clan from the town of Takrit. The efficient and brutal internal security machine was, until 1983, headed by Hussein's half-brother, Barzan Ibrahim, who was aided by two other brothers, Sabawi and Wadhban. With his cousin and brother-in-law, Adnan Khairallah, in charge of the defense portfolio, and another non-Takriti close associate of the president, Sadoun Shaker, acting as minister of the interior, Hussein was well in control of the state's instruments of coercive power.

But the reasons for Saddam Hussein's political control extended beyond the simple mechanics of state coercion. From 1976 onward, he became the architect of a variety of social welfare programs aimed at broadening his personal support base in the country. With an eye toward bridging the gap between rich and poor, he vigorously pursued policies that included massive and rapid improvements in housing, education, and medical services and enacted legislation on social security, minimum wages, and pension rights. Single-mindedly, he endeavored to change his image from that of the ruthless party man of the mid-1970s to one of a meritorious and accessible popular leader.

By the time he had assumed the presidency in 1979, in the process ruthlessly ridding himself of any possible danger to his authority, Hussein had achieved a position of clear dominance over the party.

This was more than evident in the changing attitudes of the other members of the party's command, who came to accept him as a leader rather than a mere colleague. For example, in an article in the official party newspaper, Tariq Aziz, vice president and senior member of the party leadership, wrote in an almost embarrassingly eulogistic tone:

> As for the leader of the movement, Saddam Hussein, he is not a politician who attained political authority through heredity or through rigged elections. He was the 'youth' who started his political struggle ready to martyr himself for the sake of liberation from the dictatorship of Abd al-Karim Kasim, and he is the struggler who was sentenced to death, and who led the secret military and civilian organizations of the Ba'th Party until the victorious revolution of July 1968. He is the struggler, the organizer, the thinker and the leader.[5]

No wonder, therefore, when the Ninth Regional Congress of the Ba'th Party met in June 1982, there was unanimous approval for Hussein's policies and political leadership. Not only was the Congress ecstatic about Iraq's achievements under Hussein, it also attributed every success to the president and exonerated him from any failure. The report contained much praise, most of which was directed at the president. It, thus,

> Praised the ethical leading role of Comrade Leader Saddam Hussein in rebuilding the Party—praised his historic success in leading the Party—praised his decisive and historic role in planning and implementing the revolution—praised his distinguished ability and immense courage in confronting the conspiracies against the revolution—praised his ability to plan, design and implement all the Party's prominent successes—praised his creative leadership in designing and implementing the development plan—praised [him] for leading the war (against Iran)—in all its military, strategic, mobilizational, political, economic and psychological aspects—in a creative, courageous and democratic manner.[6]

Hussein, therefore, was the dominant figure in the party and consequently in the country as a whole. Nor did he seem unduly worried about the military's potential for taking over power. The Iraq-Iran war seemed to confirm Hussein's control of the armed forces. Even when, in a war perceived to be "Hussein's war," the Iraqi armed forces were suffering the reverses that were eventually to drive them out of Iran in 1982, there was little indication that Hussein's position was threatened.

Hussein's survival at a time when many expected a possible army takeover is probably related to the increasing professionalization of the army and the mounting exasperation of the population with military interference in politics. During the sixties, Iraq experienced a succession of army coups that left the country and the armed forces weak and demoralized. Indeed, the Ba'th Party only came to power, first in 1963 and then in 1968, through military coups. The civilian members of the party had by the late 1960s realized the dangers of overreliance on the military. Thus, as early as 1966, Michel Aflaq had declared

> We hope to change the function of the army by preventing the officers from forming a bloc inside the leadership of the party. If the party selects a military member for its leadership, he should not maintain his military position, but should become a popular leader. There is no real revolutionary party in the world whose leaders are military men continuing to command army units.[7]

Saddam Hussein certainly endorsed this view and acted upon it. He, thus, declared that "with party methods, there is no chance for anyone who disagrees with us to jump on a couple of tanks and overthrow the government."[8] These party methods represented the widespread and highly successful efforts by the civilian leadership to penetrate the army with reliable party cadres. Beyond that, Hussein appointed loyal members of his own Takriti clan to sensitive command positions and ensured that army commanders were continuously reshuffled to prevent anyone from establishing a power base within the armed forces. These efforts were accompanied by effective surveillance and brutal intimidation.

In addition, Hussein and the Ba'th Party created the Popular Army in 1974 as a parallel institution to the regular armed forces. Under the command of a close associate of the president, Taha Yassin Ramadan, the membership of this basically Ba'thist militia is now estimated at around 500 thousand men and women, most of whom are party cadres. The Popular Army has been responsible for safeguarding the political leadership and has thus been used for such tasks as guarding government buildings and installations. Members usually go through a two-month annual training period, are paid directly from party funds, and are concentrated around sensitive centers. Although by no means trained as rigorously as the armed forces, the militia are in possession of sophisticated arms and are bound to weigh heavily on the calculations of ambitious or disgruntled army officers contemplating a challenge to Hussein and the political leadership.

At present, there is little doubt that it is the party that controls the army, but the civilian members of the party are the first to concede the military's role in perpetuating their political power. Hussein has tried to diminish the military's potential as a competitive interest group without making it completely depoliticized. The army, for example, is urged to see itself and act as an ideologically committed military wing of the party. All senior command positions within the army are filled by party members, and Ba'thist Party cadres are assigned to the headquarters of all units down to battalion level.

On the other hand, the president has tried to ensure that the military is well provided for materially. On his accession to the presidency, Hussein raised the salaries of all levels of the armed forces. Since the eruption of the Iraq-Iran war, the military have consistently received preferential treatment. Priority is given to members of the armed forces for car and house purchases. Frontline quarters for officers are generally lavishly equipped with beds, television sets, video machines, carpets and are furnished with direct phone lines to Iraqi cities. With these inducements complementing the pervasive party control, there seems to be, as much as one can tell, little impending threat to the regime from the defense establishment.

Hussein is the primary political personality in the country, controlling the military and keeping a very tight rein on the party. Nor does he doubt his indispensability to the party and the country. He once said in an interview that although up until 1974 he had hoped to give up power, the relationship between him and the people after 1974 developed to an extent that it made him feel that "relinquishing his responsibilities would be tantamount to abandoning the people and the party and stabbing them in the back."[9] The ubiquity of Saddam Hussein in almost every aspect of Iraqi political and social life indicates that the president practices what he believes.

Hussein's centrality was such that, by the time he had assumed the presidency in 1979, he decided to hold elections for a legislative body to be called the National Assembly. In June 1980, approximately 6 million Iraqis elected an assembly, 75 percent of whose membership was of the Ba'thist Party, including all the members of the Revolutionary Command Council (RCC) who had decided to stand. Nevertheless, 40 percent of the total assembly were Shi'ite and 12 percent Kurdish. The exercise was repeated in October 1984 with more or less the same results.

The dominance of the Ba'th was a result of a thorough screening process of all candidates. Although they did not need to be card-carrying members of the party, candidates had to declare themselves to be adherents to the principles of the 1968 Ba'thist "revolution." A commission of five high-ranking Ba'thists, under the chairmanship of an RCC member, was responsible for a painstakingly thorough arbitration of various candidates.

In theory, the assembly is supposed to have the power to propose and draft laws, to confirm the budget and plans for national development, to ratify international treaties, to debate various aspects of domestic and foreign policy, and to argue departmental performance and even to suggest the resignation of any minister. In reality, however, although some debates, whose parameters have been strictly set, have indeed taken place, the assembly's job has been restricted to endorsing policies and enacting laws submitted to it by the RCC. The assembly initiates little legislation and exercises negligible influence over the party, to say nothing of the RCC and the president. The assembly seems to have legitimated and cemented further the dominance of Saddam Hussein over other competitive personalities and institutions, including the Ba'th Party.

The Ba'th Party, however, does play a role in Iraqi politics. Because of Hussein's seeming enduring adherence to Ba'thist symbolism and his awareness of the party's important role in national mobilization, he endeavors to portray himself always as a loyal party cadre and his policies as a manifestation of party principles and goals. The relationship between the two is thus symbiotic: the party's perceived legitimacy and its organizational responsibility within the country enhances the president's power and authority, and the population's acceptance of presidential authority aids the party's status and control. In all this, however, there is little doubt that the presidency is the dominant institution.

Religion, Ethnicity, and Opposition

Strict adherence to the nationalist Ba'thist ideology has meant that Iraq has become an avowedly secularist state. Michel Aflaq, a Christian, acknowledges the debt of Arab nationalism to Islam but stresses only those aspects of Islam that are moral and spiritual in nature and pointedly disregards its political and constitutional implications. To Aflaq, Islam is important insofar as it is one of those objective characteristics that make up the Arab nation and is therefore an important segment of the Arab heritage. Aflaq insists, however, that Islam is created out of the Arab essence and therefore must be subordinate to Arab nationalism. No independent ideological status is accorded to Islam in Aflaq's scheme of things, and references to the "religion of the Arabs" are all secondary to the mainstream of his thought.

Hussein fully concurs, no doubt partly because of his Ba'thist convictions, but more important, also because of his sensitivity to the sectarian divisions within Iraq. The majority of the Arab population in Iraq belong to the Shi'ite sect of Islam, whereas political power has traditionally rested in the hands of the Sunni minority. And Hussein, a Sunni from Takrit (where a number of the present leadership originate) is naturally suspicious of "some opposition forces who seek under the cover of religion to entice the regime into interfering in religious matters which would plunge the party into the various sectarian interpretations of Islam." Hussein warns that such interference would "divide the Muslims in accordance with their varying sectarian beliefs" and asks rhetorically, "Is this not an entry into a doomed policy through its most perilous opening?"[10]

The peril of sectarianism had been gathering momentum since the early 1960s, when the hitherto quiescent Shi'ite population became more politically conscious and active. Rapid socio-economic development during this period drew large numbers of mostly tribal Shi'ites to Baghdad, where they crowded into suburban ghettos such as al-Thawra and al-Salam. While experiencing a rapid rise in their incomes, they continued to be both economically and socially second-class citizens to the Sunnis. They also suffered from high rates of inflation and a paucity of moderately priced housing. Bound by their sectarian affiliations and conscious of their relative material deprivation, they became obvious targets for revolutionary organizations, the most important of which was the al-Da'wa ("the Call") organization. Under the leadership of the learned and charismatic Ayatollah Baqr al-Sadr, al-Da'wa attracted many disaffected Shi'ites in the 1970s.

The Iranian revolution of January-February 1979 sparked al-Da'wa into a major opposition stand against the Baghdad government. In March 1980, a bomb was thrown at Tariq Aziz, the only Christian member of the Iraqi leadership, by members of al-Da'wa who, according to Baghdad, had been receiving arms, training, and equipment from Tehran. This incident and another bomb attack a few days later prompted Saddam Hussein to execute al-Sadr and to expel some 35 thousand Shi'ites, supposedly of Iranian descent, to Iran.

Acts of violence have intermittently continued since then, but the revolutionary potential of the Shi'ite community has subsided considerably for several reasons. In the first place, the loss of al-Sadr's charismatic leadership was a great blow to al-Da'wa and to the community as a whole. Secondly, the movement seems to have been fragmented and opposed by a number of indigenous Iraqi Shi'ite groups including al-Mujahidin (the Muslim Warriors) and by another organization that split off from al-Da'wa in 1980, the Munazzamat al-'Amal al-Islami (the Organization for Islamic Action). This latter group, led by Shaykh Muhammad al-Shirazi and Shaykh Hadi Mudarrisi, opposes the "adventurism" of al-Da'wa. Meanwhile, al-Da'wa itself seems to have split into two conflicting trends, one a militant fundamentalist group supporting Ayatollah Rouhallah Khomeini and the other a reformist group supporting the clerical modernists and moderates in Iran. Competing for leadership in al-Da'wa at present are Sayyid Mahdi al-Hakim and Shaykh Mahdi al-Khalisi. Competition for leadership is further complicated by splits between those ulama of Persian and Arab extraction. Third, the atrocities of the Iranian revolution have greatly dampened the early euphoria and have convinced many Iraqi Shi'ites that a clerical alternative to Saddam Hussein may not be all that attractive. Finally, the president's massive social welfare program, begun in the late 1970s, benefited the Shi'ite population far more than any other community, because the Shi'ites constituted the bulk of Iraq's poor.

One consolation of an otherwise disastrous war with Iran was that Iraqi demographic unity seemed able to withstand the enticements of the Iranian clergy. Only six months after the eruption of hostilities, it had become clear that the Iraqi Shi'ites were not going to revolt against the Baghdad Sunni government, and that, contrary to the promises of the ayatollahs, the dislocation of the Iraqi army—the vast majority of whose rank and file was Shi'ites—was far from imminent. With obvious relief, Saddam Hussein declared that while there were "Sunnis, Shi'ites and other religions and sects in Iraq," it was "the unified Iraqi people who were fighting the war."[11]

Even so, the Iraqi secularist leaders could not but be sensitive to the cultural ubiquity of Islam. They calculated that it would be prudent to allude increasingly to religious symbolism. As the war progressed, the president and other party leaders were seen attending mosque prayers more regularly than in the period before the war. The streets began to be filled with pictures of the president with Qur'an in hand or reverently kneeling in humble prayer. The frequency of Qur'anic recitals, as well as of religious discussion, on radio and television increased. More significantly, government disbursements toward the building of new mosques were raised considerably. This was particularly the case with the regime's funding for the Shi'ite holy places in Karbala, which between 1974 and 1981 had received $80 million. In 1982 alone, however, the regime's allocation for Karbala amounted to $24 million, while a further $24 million was earmarked for the other Shi'ite holy city of Najaf, where, for example, the inner shrine of al-Haydariya mosque was lavished with gold and silver leaf. In addition to marble work and crystal chandeliers, the two big mosques in Karbala, where the tombs of Imam Hussein and Imam Abbas lie, were installed with power generators and air-conditioning. In light of this, the Iraqi semiofficial newspaper, *al-Thawra*, attacked the Iranian leaders for accusing Iraq of being anti-Islamic. The paper retorted

> We tell you that Iraq is a true Islamic state, and the people of Iraq, as well as its leaders, believe in God and in the teachings of Islam as a religion and as a heritage. Indeed President Hussein's regular visits to the holy shrines and his continuous efforts to provide for these shrines is a clear proof of his deep and unequivocal belief in the glorious message of Islam.[12]

Beyond the efforts to portray himself and his colleagues as good Muslims, the president, aware of his Sunni affiliations, consciously and frequently referred reverently to the early leaders of Shi'ite Islam, Ali and Hussein. In an emotional speech in the Shi'ite city of Najaf, he declared

> We shall never tire of making sacrifices as long as we know that right is on our side; as long as we know that God is with us. Today, our great ancestor, the father of all martyrs, Hussein, may God's peace be upon him, stands as a lofty symbol of heroism, glory and firmness in defending right. . . . We, his descendants, are proud to be connected with him; we are proud to be tied to him in soul and blood. We are fighting to defend right, justice and the holy land of Iraq which harbors the remains of our ancestor Ali, may God brighten his face.[13]

In this passage, Hussein skillfully counteracted Iranian claims that he was an infidel and an enemy of Islam by his deference to Iraq's Islamic heritage; by his respect for, and loyalty to, the two main symbols of Shi'ite Islam; and by reminding his listeners that it was they, the Arabs, and not the Iranians, who were the descendants of Ali and Hussein.

Iraqi-Iranian relations touched on another serious demographic problem inside Iraq, namely the Kurdish question. Ethnically non-Arab and inhabiting the oil-rich lands of northern Iraq, the Kurds had, since the birth of the modern Iraqi state in the 1920s, demanded a state of their own. When the new Ba'thist government came to power in 1968, Iraq had been almost drained militarily and financially by a Kurdish rebellion that had continued throughout the 1960s. The

Ba'thist leaders first tried to suppress the rebellion but were unsuccessful. In March 1970, therefore, a settlement with the Kurds was reached that incorporated many of the Kurdish demands.

Delays in implementing the agreement led to the reactivation of the rebellion, so that by autumn 1974, almost 60 thousand Iraqi troops were engaged in the north of Iraq fighting an almost invisible guerrilla force in a difficult mountainous terrain. The shah of Iran, in conflict with the Iraqi Ba'thists over the Shatt al-Arab waterway and other border disputes, vigorously aided the Kurdish military resistance with vital arms supplies and, later on in the year, with the actual involvement of Iranian artillery and air force. The Baghdad government clearly saw that only through acceding to Iranian demands would Iraq be able to defeat the Kurds. In March 1975, the shah and Saddam Hussein met in Algiers and signed an agreement that ended border disputes to the satisfaction of Tehran in return for an Iranian pledge to end all support for the Kurds. Almost immediately, the Kurdish rebellion collapsed, and the Iraqi armed forces took over complete control of the north of Iraq.

Kurdish resentment, however, persisted, and the Kurds' perception of themselves as a distinct and separate ethnic group deserving of a national home did not subside. As such, they continued to constitute a matter of grave concern to the central government in Baghdad, particularly after the eruption of the Iraq-Iran war in 1980, when Iraq needed to move troops from the north to the southern border with Iran. In the early 1980s, government control over the Kurdish areas in the north of Iraq began to diminish. The Kurds continue to disrupt food traffic between Iraq and Turkey, and they seem to control, particularly at night, large areas around the northern cities of Kirkuk, Arbil, and Sulaymaniyah. Fortunately for Iraq, the Kurds are racked by internal factionalism, and, as Sunnis, they have received even harsher treatment and persecution at the hands of the Iranian Shi'ite clergy.

The authorities in Baghdad, nevertheless, cannot discount a possible resurgence of a widespread Kurdish rebellion. Nor can they ignore the possibility of a future dislocation in Iraq's delicate demographic balance or social strains imposed on the country by a fragile war economy. In addition, the obstinacy of the Iranian clergy means that the Iraqi leaders can see no end in sight to the disastrous war with Iran. A leadership less confidently in control would have long since collapsed under the weight of such heavy burdens. Saddam Hussein and the Ba'th Party, however, have survived the onslaught well. Will they survive the next one or two decades equally well, or will they finally succumb to the gathering domestic and external forces? To predict one or the other of these eventualities is a reckless endeavor. But it can be argued that in the absence of a dramatic military or economic collapse, or a successful assassination of the president, there is every reason to believe that Saddam Hussein and the Ba'th Party can survive the next decade or two through using the same methods that have served them so well so far: ruthlessness and coercion on the one hand; populist appeal, material inducements, and ideological mobilization on the other.

Notes

1. Quoted in Majid Khadduri, *Socialist Iraq: A Study in Iraqi Politics since 1968* (Washington, D.C.: The Middle East Institute, 1978), 208.

2. Ibid., 207.

3. *Guardian* (London), May 22, 1972.

4. Documents of the Third Congress of the Iraqi Communist Party (in Arabic) (Baghdad: ICP, 1976), 48.

5. *Al-Thawra* (Baghdad), May 9, 1980.

6. British Broadcasting Corporation, *Summary of World Broadcasts*, ME/7066/A/10, July 1, 1982.

7. *Al-Hayat* (Beirut), February 25, 1966.

8. *Guardian* (London), November 26, 1971.

9. *Al-Thawra* (Baghdad), December 28, 1982.

10. Saddam Hussein, "Hawla Kitabat al-Tarikh" ("On Writing History"), in *Al-Turath al-Arabi wal Mu'asara (Arab Heritage and Contemporary Life)* by Saddam Hussein (Baghdad: Dar al-Huriya, 1978), 9.

11. *Al-Thawra* (Baghdad), March 3, 1981.

12. *Al-Thawra* (Baghdad), January 16, 1982.

13. *Al-Thawra* (Baghdad), April 2, 1982.

3

Economic Outlook:
Guns and Butter, Phase Two?

Jonathan Crusoe

During its war with Iran, Iraq's economy has undergone numerous significant changes. Development expenditures have risen and fallen dramatically in comparison with prewar levels, and long-range planning was until recently replaced by the adoption of tentative year-to-year budgets. Nevertheless, Iraq's economy retains a resilient vitality. In October 1985, a new pipeline spur linking Iraq's southern oil fields with Saudi Arabia's Red Sea port of Yanbu was commissioned. Baghdad is optimistic that this project and the planned expansion of the export pipeline through Turkey will help solve its most pressing economic problems.

Chief among these problems has been an inability to meet debt repayments owed to several countries, including Japan, India, and West Germany, which were deferred in 1983. Baghdad is hoping that increased revenue from the pipelines will improve its repayment record, as well as boosting foreign confidence. According to First Deputy Prime Minister Taha Yassin Ramadan, "The end of 1985 will mark the end of all difficulties and the payment of all debts."

In addition, a new five-year plan is to be launched in 1986. "We are going ahead in developing our economic resources despite the conditions of the war," Iraqi President Saddam Hussein has said of the plan.[1] It is expected to concentrate on social services, as well as continuing development of the oil industry and the agricultural sector. According to Deputy Prime Minister Ramadan, the government has actually prepared two parallel development plans, one assuming that the war will end within two years and the other assuming that it will continue indefinitely.[2] Outside observers are well advised to note further developments as the country begins the second half-decade of the war.

The Early War Economy

At the start of 1981, four months after the war with Iran had begun, Iraq embarked on the 1981–1985 five-year development plan with an expenditure estimated at around $130 billion. Despite Baghdad's determination to continue its program of economic development, the tremendous cost of the war—both in money and manpower—has caused severe disruptions as the country has struggled to come to terms with its lack of foreign currency. Once, it seemed inconceivable that Iraq would ever be short of money. Before the war started, oil exports stood at between 2.5–3 million barrels per day (b/d), estimated income was around $26 billion, and reserves had been built up to the $35 billion mark. Now, very little of this reserve remains, and Iraq, once proud of its reputation as a cash payer, relies on credit to a great extent.

In retrospect, 1981 proved a disastrous year domestically. In a seemingly strong financial position and having a clear determination to continue development despite the war, Baghdad launched its five-year plan by awarding contracts worth some $20 billion for new project work. Imports, which had been rising in step with higher oil revenues, from $10.6 billion in 1979 to $16.5 billion in 1980, reached $18.7 billion in 1981. But now income was drying up rapidly. Iraq's two offshore oil export terminals in the Gulf had been badly damaged at the start of the war by Iranian attacks, and oil revenues were plummeting to an estimated $10.5 billion for the year. Meanwhile, the cost of fighting the war was also increasing. By 1982, it was estimated to cost around $1 billion a month. By way of comparison, war costs are now estimated at up to $5 billion a year.

Baghdad straightforwardly sought financial help. At the beginning of 1983, the government admitted that friendly Arab countries—Saudi Arabia, Kuwait, the United Arab Emirates (UAE) and Qatar—had loaned up to $25 billion, and Saudi Arabia and Kuwait were also helping by supplying their oil to Iraqi customers. But the money was not enough, and at the beginning of 1982, a moratorium on the award of new contracts was declared, except for war-related and priority projects. Unfortunately, just as the Reagan administration succeeded in removing Iraq from the list of countries accused of supporting terrorism—a first step toward normalizing trade relations—President Saddam Hussein announced a period of austerity.

For contractors who had benefited from the spate of awards in 1980–1981, times became worrisome. Although they had been assured in May 1982 that they would enjoy financial priority, this was clearly not the case by the end of the year. There had already been cases where contracts had been awarded but not signed, and reports that contractors bidding for several large projects had been advised to put together financing packages. In November 1982, the Baghdad municipality informed contractors working on a major housing scheme in the capital that they should consider the possibility of finding their own sources of credit to finance the rest of their work.

The drain of payments to contractors was such that by February 1983, most clients (government ministries) had announced that companies must refinance the foreign currency portion of payments due that year. Baghdad's blunt message, as summed up by Foreign Affairs Minister Tariq Aziz, was: "If you want to liquidate your contracts, then we are prepared to do this and we will shoulder the burden. If you wish to continue the work, then you must provide resources to continue the work on reasonable terms."[3] International contractors, generally facing a shrinking world market, and in many cases with massive investment of plant and equipment in Iraq, had little choice. Most accepted the situation, albeit at terms that probably proved more "reasonable" to Baghdad than to themselves.

Some contractors chose not to continue, however, and there are still court cases pending involving companies that pulled out when payments were not met according to the contract and bid bonds were in turn called by the client. The pressure was intense. Foreign currency payments were in some cases already more than three months in arrears by the beginning of 1983; dinar payments, although made on time, were almost worthless outside the country. Clients had little cash and were forced to play for time. Contract extensions were negotiated and, in some cases, performance certificates were not signed—a practice that still prevails.

1983: Year of Adjustment

But during the course of 1983, most companies came to some agreement with their clients. Some, like the French and Indians, were covered by government-to-government negotiations. The West German government left its contractors to sort out their own problems, as did the United Kingdom (UK). Japanese deferrals were negotiated through the three main trading houses operating in Iraq, the Mitsubishi, Marubeni, and Sumitomo corporations. The terms usually consisted of Iraq agreeing to pay up to 10 percent of foreign currency payments due that year, with the remainder to be deferred for two years. The Indians agreed to take oil and sulfur as partial payment, and some South Korean companies and the Japanese took oil in payment for 1982 debts. Other sources of credit were also being investigated.

Baghdad went to the Euromarket and signed a $500 million loan at the end of March 1983—the Chase Manhattan Bank and Irving Trust Company were among bank participants. Jordan and Turkey made short-term credit available to cover imports.

The government, of necessity, sought tighter control over expenditure, and the Central Bank of Iraq maintained strict ceilings on spending. Imports declined sharply to the $8–10 billion level, and the authorities pressed for up to 18 months credit for all imports. Even the Defense Ministry prefered two years credit for certain items. The government also introduced a scheme to defer for two years the dollar payments to Filipinos working in the state sector—an estimated $4 billion was leaving the country every year in remittance payments for expatriate workers.

Domestically, workers were urged to increase productivity levels. There was increased dependence on locally made products and export markets were sought for any surplus. The private sector was encouraged to play a wider role. In Baghdad, payment by American Express Card in the major hotels was introduced to stop the widespread practice of visitors buying dinars cheaply outside the country to pay their hotel bills. A spontaneous campaign of donations—so successful that it was eventually officially encouraged by the government— realized several hundred million dollars worth of cash, gold, jewelry, and property.

The clearest indication of Baghdad's plight was the news that two loans had been made by the Arab Monetary Fund to support the country's balance of payments. Other Arab financial institutions were also approached, and loans were signed with the Islamic Development Bank and the Arab Fund for Economic and Social Development.

European and Japanese Credits

To date, Iraq has been successful in getting credit to fund imports and a certain amount of project work. Its immediate neighbors, Jordan and Turkey, have offered credit terms to finance imports since it first became clear that Iraq was in financial difficulties. Equally important, however, was the apparent willingness of West European countries to offer credit.

Austria and the United Kingdom were the first to make such credit publicly available in 1983. The UK offered a total of $362 million made up of a general-purpose line of credit for nominated capital goods and equipment, a buyer credit for project work—used for power stations, housing, hospital, water supply, and oil projects— and a loan for pharmaceutical projects. The latter was used up first.

In 1985, a new British loan was offered, structured along the same lines but with an increased portion for pharmaceuticals.

Austrian companies are still being awarded contracts—two in the first half of 1985—under a $268 million credit set up by Vienna. Italy has made up to $500 million available in credit and has also said it is prepared to support contracts on a case by case basis, as is France. Greece, too, has agreed to make export credit available for development projects and has put up $100 million in credit facilities for traded goods. Ireland now operates a $24 million roll-over credit with no fixed term. Once repayment on a specific project has been made, the money becomes available for another company.

The availability of credit from the Eastern bloc is not clear, although East Germany has offered some $200 million to support project work and the supply of capital goods. The Soviet Union has also put up $2 billion in long-term credit at minimal interest rates, although this may be tied to specific oil and power generation projects. Yugoslavia, politically and economically close to Baghdad, has offered $500 million in financing for new work. It has also taken oil in partial payment for moneys due, as have some other East European countries, France, Japan, and some individual companies.

In 1983, Baghdad also succeeded in persuading Japan to reextend $1.8 billion in grants and loans originally offered in the mid-1970s. While the war continues and while Japanese firms are still owed large amounts of money, however, Tokyo has been unwilling to commit money for large projects and to date has only officially extended credit to support the purchase of medical equipment for 13 Japanese-built hospitals and construction of a fertilizer project.

Other countries have been prepared to defer payments, in some cases for up to two years, to sell their products and maintain their markets. Australia, Canada, and Brazil have sold wheat and meat on such terms, and since 1982, when the U.S. Department of Agriculture began granting credit guarantees to enable Iraq to buy cereals and other agricultural products, the Commodities Credit Corporation (CCC) had, by the end of its fiscal year 1985, built up exposure of approximately $1.8 billion.

1985: A Critical Year

In the view of its foreign creditors, 1985 was anticipated as a crucial year for Baghdad. The key question was whether the economy had been managed sufficiently well to accumulate enough foreign exchange to meet repayments deferred since 1983. Foreign Minister Tariq Aziz certainly had no doubts, giving assurances in Washington in November 1984, that obligations arising from deferred payment deals struck in the past would be met in full, and that there would be no further reschedulings. "Whatever was delayed, or rescheduled in 1983 in order to be paid in 1985 will be paid, dollar for dollar."[4]

But by the beginning of 1985, Iraq's total indebtedness was estimated at around $40 billion. Of this, at least $25 billion was loaned by friendly Arab states and is unlikely to be paid for some years, if ever. Apart from military debt and oil owed to Kuwait and Saudi Arabia, which have been supplying Iraqi customers with up to 350 thousand b/d from the Divided Zone since 1983, there is a large portion of civil debt owed to contractors and suppliers. For 1985 the amount owed was estimated at some $1 billion, with probably a further $3 billion due in 1986.

In March and October 1985, Iraq met—on time—the first and second installments on payments deferred by France in 1983, and on the $500 million Euroloan raised in 1983, a total of $442 million. A further five semi-annual payments of $71 million are due on the Euroloan, and four semi-annual payments of $150 million are due to France, which agreed to defer about $1 billion in 1983. Priority has clearly been accorded to meeting bank debt and payments due to the French. But ominous signs that foreign exchange remained short were confirmed by Oil Minister Qassem Ahmad Taqi when he said, "It is true that we are trying to reschedule several loans, because in 1985 we are passing through a critical financial and economic period compared with previous and future years."[5] He added that while military and other import requirements remain much the same, additional obligations have resulted from payments deferred in 1983–1984. "This accumulation of commitments cannot be made out of our current resources," he said.[6]

Thus, although the Iraqis were on time with the first installment (about $95 million) on a total of $340 million deferred by West Germany in 1983, the second installment was not met. Baghdad also informed India and Japan that it would be unable to meet repayments due in 1985 and requested a further two-year deferment. The Japanese eventually agreed, while the West Germans undertook to sell Iraqi crude oil in an attempt to cover a portion of its outstanding payments. The precise impact on other countries and companies remains unclear, but East Germany and Yugoslavia have indicated that they will take oil in lieu of 1985 moneys due from deferment agreements reached in 1983.

Meanwhile, contractors still working in Iraq have had to defer 1985 payments for two years. Over the last couple of years, the contractors have been subjected to a series of government statements advising them not to desert Iraq. In mid-1983, Tariq Aziz described the attractive prospects that the future offered: "Most of the countries we have been dealing with all know how strong the Iraqi economy is and how great the resources are, and trust the Iraqi future."[7] The real message was again more blunt; both President Saddam Hussein and First Deputy Premier Taha Yassin Ramadan warned foreign governments and companies that they will not be treated favorably if they treat Iraq negatively. Ramadan has continued to stress this message, and it is reported in the daily *Baghdad Observer* whenever he meets visiting delegations. Perseverance will bring "priority concessions." Companies that "showed reluctance" and "fell short in their commitment to Iraq (have) damaged their own interests as they will miss future opportunities," he said in late 1984.[8]

The suggestion is that, assuming the war will eventually end, there will be a boom perhaps comparable to the golden days of 1981. This boom would be fueled by the substantially increased revenues resulting from new export pipelines through Turkey and Saudi Arabia. Completion of the second Turkish line and the two-phase Saudi line would enable an export flow of about 3.1 million b/d—at full capacity—between mid-1987 and mid-1988. But it is considered unlikely that Iraq will be allowed to sell more than 2 million b/d whatever special case it might plead to OPEC, and the additional revenue accruing will be used to fund the war, to repay debts, and to meet import bills, rather than to fund a massive new development program. The aftermath of the 1981 spending proved a sobering experience for the government and one that it will not wish to repeat, even if the war were to end in the near future.

Sectoral Analysis

On the surface Iraq's development prospects have looked promising, with its large population (now estimated at about 15 million), large reserves of oil, and some 12 million hectares of cultivable land and water. But development up to the late 1970s was limited not by shortages of capital, but by the country's small absorbtive capacity, together with ineffective planning and poor administration.

Since the early 1970s, Iraq's development strategy has been aimed at industrial diversification, agricultural self-sufficiency, infrastructural development, and improvements in social services and education, while attempting to move away from an oil-based economy. The 1976–1980 five-year plan envisaged spending a total of Iraqi dinar (ID) 13.6 billion, with industry getting the greatest share (32 percent), followed by agriculture (18.7 percent), transport and communications

(17.5 percent), and buildings and services (16.9 percent). No break-downs are available for the 1981–1985 plan; however, total spending was forecast at some $130 billion, with priority accorded to services—housing, water, electricity, health, and education—transport, communications, and industry. Because of the war, Baghdad has replaced the five-year program with an annual investment plan.

The Petroleum Sector

With the financial problems of 1982–1983 came a rethinking of priorities and, above all, a determination to make more efficient use of the country's available resources. Chief among these resources is oil, which funded 80 percent of the 1976–1980 plan. In the 1980s, oil still accounted for some 65 percent of the gross domestic product (GDP), with agriculture and industry each accounting for between 7 and 8 percent and services, for 19 percent. Iraq has massive oil reserves, estimated at least at 100 billion barrels, with 65 billion proven. The main fields are in the north around Kirkuk and in the south at Rumaila and are linked by the north-south strategic pipeline that can pump oil in either direction.

At least six new oil fields have been identified at Majnoun, Nahr-Umr, Qurna, Halfaya, East Baghdad, and West Baghdad. One of the largest of these fields is Majnoun, where reserves are estimated at 7 billion barrels, with an expected production capacity of about 700 thousand b/d. Brazil's Braspetro discovered Majnoun in 1976 and provided the subsequent engineering and technical services. The field's future is in doubt, however, following Iranian incursions into the area in 1984. Braspetro will also provide technical assistance at another southern oil field, Nahr-Umr, which is believed to contain reserves of 1 billion barrels.

Technical services for development of Iraq's other new fields have been negotiated with a wide variety of other companies and countries. The Soviet Union is to assist in developing the Basra governorate's field at Qurna; it signed an agreement in February 1985 that points to the possible setting up of production facilities. The Soviets are also working on second stage development of the north Rumaila field to increase production to an average 800 thousand b/d. Italy's ENI and its subsidiary Agip Petroli are responsible for the Halfaya field in the Misan governorate, while France's CFP-Total and Mobil Oil of the United States have supplied technical services for the East and West Baghdad fields. Work on East Baghdad began in late 1984 with the award of a pilot degassing scheme to Italy's Snamprogetti. This field's reserves are estimated at up to 10.5 billion barrels. Overall, these six new fields could increase Iraq's production capacity from the prewar total of 4 million b/d to some 6 million b/d.

These activities notwithstanding, the main focus of investment in the oil sector has been in new pipeline facilities, for strategic as well as economic reasons. Before the war, Iraq had 4.5 million b/d in export capacity through its offshore Gulf terminals at Khor al-Amaya and Mina al-Bakr. Both facilities were extensively damaged by Iranian attacks, and after the pipeline across Syria was closed in April 1982, only the pipeline through Turkey remained. It was clear to Baghdad that its Gulf outlets would always be too vulnerable to rely on completely and that while Kurdish guerrillas were active in the north, the Turkish pipeline would always be liable to attack. Baghdad sought alternative routes, across Saudi Arabia to the Red Sea port of Yanbu, and across Jordan to its main port of Aqaba. U.S. firms have been involved with both lines—Brown & Root is the engineer for the Saudi route, and Bechtel has been responsible for planning the Jordan line. Italian and French contractors have completed the $500 million first stage of the Saudi line that links Iraq's southern oil fields with the Saudi's east-west Petroline, and it was expected to be pumping up to 500 thousand b/d by the end of 1985. Talks about a second stage have been under way for some time. This stage would involve building a new pipeline across Saudi Arabia to Yanbu (total costs are estimated at around $2 billion) and would give Iraq an additional 1.6 million b/d of export capacity, probably by mid-1988.

The $950 million, 1 million b/d pipeline to Aqaba continues to be a subject of discussion between Bechtel and Baghdad. The latter is still insisting on guarantees of relief from payment for work on the pipeline if the flow of oil through the line were to be stopped by third party intervention, notably Israel. Despite this, Iraq is understood to be keen to retain the Jordanian option, and the project therefore cannot be described as dead. In addition, the U.S. EXIM Bank has made a preliminary commitment to support the $570 million U.S portion of the project.

EXIM Bank also agreed in principle to make available $112 million in export credits for U.S.-source components that might be used on Iraq's third pipeline project—a new line parallel to the existing line through Turkey. This contract has been awarded to an Italian-Turkish consortium of Saipem, Tekfen and Kutlutas. Once it is completed in early 1987, the line will export some 1.5 million b/d in tandem with the other trans-Turkey line.

Iraq's reliance on oil exports is also poignantly reflected in a large-scale program to truck oil products through Jordan and Turkey. Such exports may have reached as high as 80 thousand b/d after being boosted by the commissioning of the 150 thousand b/d Ba'iji refinery in 1983. A new 250 thousand b/d lube oil refinery is now also being built in Ba'iji by a French-Italian group. An export refinery, with capacity of up to 250 thousand b/d, has been planned for some time; one has been designed by the M. W. Kellogg Company for Nasiriyah, but this is now likely to be built at Haditha, west of Baghdad.

There have also been plans to expand production and promote natural gas for domestic use and export. In 1980, the country was producing about 11.37 billion cubic meters of gas a day, of which 9.61 billion cubic meters a day was flared. Large gas-gathering schemes have been set up to use up to 80 percent of gas production for domestic and industrial purposes. Tenders have been invited for an NLG/LPG plant to be built northwest of Basra. Italy's Snamprogetti has designed a 3 million-ton-a-year pipeline to export natural gas through Turkey. This has now been shelved as Iraq says its gas reserves are not sufficient to invest in such a scheme yet. A natural gas pipeline may be built from Kirkuk to Turkey's Batman refinery, however. Iraq may also be looking to establish underground storage for gas, both in the north and south. There are also plans to build a pipeline to supply natural gas to Kuwait.

Industrial and Infrastructural Development

Refined oil products and chemical products had already outstripped dates as Iraq's most important non-oil export before the war started. Basra's giant petrochemical complex number 1, built by a U.S.-West German joint venture of Lummus and Thyssen, would have increased such exports had the war not broken out just as commissioning was due to take place. There is also considerable potential for sales of sulfur, of which Iraq has large reserves, and chemical fertilizers. Already self-sufficient in fertilizers, Iraq's position as an exporter should improve once the phosphate fertilizer complex at Al Qa'im becomes fully operational.

As a result of huge investment during 1979–1981 in cement, brick, and formwork factories—primarily to feed its own massive construction program—Iraq is now exporting building materials. In 1984 cement exports increased to some 2.5 million tons to Gulf countries and 24 thousand tons to Jordan. Cement production is now up to around 8 million tons a year and is expected to reach 22 million tons a year by the end of 1986. The Trade Ministry also expects to be exporting asbestos pipes and sheets, tiles, and mosaics. The ministry forecast a 104 percent increase in non-oil exports for 1985, as a result of increases in productive capacities of the sulfur, fertilizer, cement, and electric goods industries. Other exports include dry batteries, light bulbs, air coolers, electric fans, soaps, cosmetics, and medical and pharmaceutical products.

Local industry has benefited from Baghdad's determination to continue investment in industrial projects on which work was already under way when the cash shortage became apparent and that are now being commissioned. There has also been an emphasis on supporting locally manufactured products, with priority being given to meeting local industry's demands for raw materials, spare parts, and new machinery and equipment, a policy that is likely to continue. Notable as well is that foodstuffs, beverages, and the tobacco industry accounted for 31 percent of manufacturing output in 1981, a reflection on the 1976–1980 plan's emphasis on establishing consumer and light industries.

The efforts to encourage the industrial sector, particularly manu-facturing industries, to play an effective role in financing future development is also a direct result of the ninth regional conference of the ruling Arab Ba'th Socialist Party held in June 1982. There, the industrial sector came in for severe criticism, in particular for low levels of production and low technical standards, especially in middle management. By early 1984, Taha Yassin Ramadan stated that "It is essential for the ministries concerned to . . . increase production and manpower performance, and make available all the latest equipment and factories, and operate them ideally."[9]

Another criticism made in 1982 was that industrial growth had outstripped infrastructural development, a situation that was certainly apparent in 1979–1980 when contractors experienced severe delays in receiving building material and equipment imported from abroad. The ports could not cope with the massive demand—there was severe congestion—and the country's distribution network was unable to cope with the traffic. One Japanese trading house found it necessary to build its own berth. Considerable investment was planned to expand the country's two ports at Basra and Umm Qasr. Basra's future role as a major port now looks extremely limited, however, and any further port investment is likely to be at Umm Qasr, less vulnerable to Iranian attacks, where there is a large backlog of work shelved since the start of the war.

Recognizing that the country's short coastline is likely to remain vulnerable, the government has implemented several large road and rail projects under a program to improve both internal links as well as connections with neighboring countries through which imports have poured since the start of the war. Projects include the $3 billion expressway number 1, a six-lane highway that will link Baghdad with

Syria, Jordan, and Kuwait. A similar highway is being planned between the capital and the Turkish border.

Wherever possible, all major industrial projects are to be linked with the rail network on which Brazilian, Indian, and South Korean companies have been working. The largest rail project, which links Baghdad with the Syrian border at Husaiba via the phosphate mines at Akashat mines at Al Qa'im, is due to open in late 1985. The Iraqis have put an operations and management contract for the line out to tender. New lines have been designed to run between Baghdad and Basra, and eventually to the Kuwaiti border, and north from Baghdad to the Turkish border, where connection to the Turkish network has been under discussion for some time. At one point it looked as though the Iraqis would press ahead with implementation of the Baghdad-Basra line, but its cost and proximity to the war front have deferred these plans. Also planned is a loop line system around Baghdad, into which all lines would run, and a large new freight terminal was also to be built in the capital. As early as 1979, Iraqi ministers were talking of the country as being a major transit center for goods bound from Europe to the Gulf. Links with Gulf road and rail networks will eventually make this possible.

About $1.3 billion has been spent on new international airports at Baghdad, where chaos (compared with the old airport) has since been at a minimum, and at Basra, where work has been hampered by the war. Development of a third international airport at Mosul is also stalled. The war has also delayed plans to develop a river transport system between Basra and Baghdad, and eventually Mosul, up and down the Tigris.

The Agricultural Sector

Saddam Hussein was once fond of saying that agriculture is "permanent oil." The goal of self-sufficiency has been the aim of successive five-year agricultural plans, an objective which has always been potentially within Iraq's reach. The Tigris-Euphrates river system creates a basin that has been described as one of the largest potential agricultural areas in the world. Some 12 million hectares (of Iraq's total land area of 43 million hectares) are cultivable. Performance of the agricultural sector has remained disappointing, however, and food imports continue to rise at a time when the country can ill afford them.

One of the main problems that Iraq has been struggling to overcome has been excessive soil salinity. It was estimated in the early 1950s that about 65 percent of irrigated land had been affected by salinity.

By the early 1970s, an estimated 20-30 percent of cultivated land in irrigated areas had been abandoned because of high concentrations of salt. As a result, the government has initiated a program of land reclamation, installing new and more efficient irrigation and drainage systems. By 1985, 3.5 million hectares are to have been reclaimed, rising to 4.4 million hectares by 2000. Many projects are huge: the Dujayl agro-industrial project, set up by the Yugoslavs, is eventually intended to produce some 22 percent of Iraq's total output of crops and animal products. Reclamation work is also under way on three other large schemes: 300 thousand hectares at Kirkuk, 270 thousand hectares at Abu Ghraib, and work has just been started by South Korean and Chinese contractors on the first stage of the Al Jazirah scheme that will eventually reclaim 100 thousand hectares. Several equally large programs have been postponed by the war.

Baghdad is determined to go ahead with its water control and storage program, despite delays caused by the war. Bids have been placed for two large dams, which together are expected to cost around $2.5–$3 billion. The Chinese have picked up two large contracts to build river barrages to store water for irrigation. The policy to establish more effective control over water resources has already paid dividends. In the summer of 1984, the government was able to release stored water to offset the low levels of the Euphrates. Concern over Syrian and Turkish plans to build dams on the Tigris and Euphrates should be partially offset once the Mosul and Haditha dams have been completed, probably in 1986.

Over the last few years, the government has done much to encourage local farmers by introducing more mechanization and making generous loans available from the Agricultural Cooperative Bank. It has not, however, been able to halt the urban drift, which in 1960–1981 caused the rural proportion of the population to drop from 57 to 28 percent, leaving only about 3.8 million living in the countryside. The problems have stemmed from the top. Inconsistent policies brought no improvement to a notoriously inefficient rural bureaucracy. Local financial, technical, and marketing organizations were weak. As a result, cultivation practices were unimproved, production was low, and incomes were depressed.

As a result, the agricultural sector also came in for severe criticism at the June 1982 Ba'th Party conference. Despite "revolutionary and radical" changes carried out by the party, there were still problems and drawbacks: "most important were the state's involvement in smaller parts of agricultural production and the bureaucratic practices of the state's organs concerned—both of which were stumbling blocks to the growth and improvement of production."[10] The state, the conference said, was unable to respond to the practical needs of small farmers and should focus its attention on large-scale farmers and on large-scale, vital projects. Even state farms were criticised: "The state carried out certain agricultural projects in the form of state and collective farms which are economically worthless. They have burdened the agricultural sector instead of contributing to development—such problems must be overcome."[11] Shortages of trained staff and organizational weaknesses were also highlighted.

The conference report also stated that the private sector should also be left to its own initiatives "within a non-exploiting ownership." In 1983, a new law was introduced to encourage local and Arab companies and individuals to rent reclaimed land. Loans and subsidies were available from the state bank and farmers could export their produce. Farmers were also allowed to sell directly to public-sector wholesale markets, bypassing the State Organization for Agricultural Marketing. The latter now faces a limited form of competition from a mixed-sector company—the Iraqi Company for Agricultural Products Marketing—that announced its first tenders in 1985. These criticisms of the state-run agricultural sector were endorsed publicly by Taha Yassin Ramadan at the beginning of 1984, when he stated that the government was no longer prepared to tolerate unprofitable state farms and that it was "no longer an obligation" to belong to a farmer's cooperative or a state farm. He added, "farmers must be given a greater degree of freedom to cultivate the land in a way they think suitable and most profitable."[12]

Encouragement of the Private Sector

The 1982 conference was a landmark for the private sector. It was then that the ruling Arab Ba'th Socialist Party recognized "both the legitimacy and the importance of the private sector in the economic field."[13] Taha Yassin Ramadan subsequently added that the "political and ideological objections of public ownership of means of production need not stand in the way of promoting private capital in industry."[14] This was official recognition of the private and mixed sectors' ability to meet vital consumer needs more efficiently than the state.

At the beginning of 1984, Trade Minister Hassan Ali announced that the private sector would play a larger role in economic development. Substantial increases in budget allocations for the private sector were planned, especially for the process of production of essential commodities. It was deemed necessary that egg production could be increased to cut back on imports, private poultry farmers were instructed to switch to egg production. The private sector was also seen as a solution to other problems. In 1984, private investors were given permission to set and run 16 petrol-filling stations around Baghdad; despite Iraq's oil wealth, there is a surprising shortage of filling stations. In mid-1984, the final endorsement was made by Saddam Hussein, when he admitted that "we cannot imagine a better life without a flourishing private sector in industry, agriculture, commerce, and services."[15] The state will continue to exercise ultimate control, however, and Taha Yassin Ramadan has warned that the sector should remember that the basic aim should not be "exorbitant profit at the expense of their countrymen."[16]

Public Services

A determination to improve standards in the health service has also included incentives offered to private doctors to set up hospitals. Government-backed loans and tax exemptions are available as well as permission to recruit 20 percent of the staff from abroad. The government's goal of "health for all" by 2000 has brought continuing investment in building new hospitals throughout the war. The Japanese have built and equipped 13 400-bed general hospitals, and a series of children's and maternity hospitals have been built by Spanish and French companies. The huge Baghdad medical complex, designed by Rogers, Burgun, Shahine & Deschler of the United States, has also been completed. A rehabilitation hospital has recently been opened in Tikrit, and such services for the war-wounded have increased. Staffing remains a problem, however. Too many doctors have been drafted, and in 1983 it was admitted that 10 thousand more nurses would be needed to provide for the future expansion of the health service. Only one hospital—the Ibn al-Batar in Baghdad—is run by a foreign company, Ireland's PARC Hospital Management. The hospital offers specialist services, and the government considers the investment worthwhile, saving scarce foreign currency by treating patients at home rather than sending them abroad. Other new hospitals appear to be run by staff transferred from older hospitals.

Attention to health reflects the government's broader desire to improve social services. A wide scale and compulsory anti-illiteracy campaign was started in 1979, and a large program for building schools is under way to cope with the increasing school-age population. Also, emphasis is placed on vocational training to improve technical standards. At least two new universities are being designed, but the expansion program for Baghdad, Mosul, Basra, and the technological university have been delayed by the war. The housing program has also been set back. Implementation of plans to build a total of 3.4

million new homes by 2000 has been slowed. Much of the work is now being done by the State Organization for Housing.

One of the few sectors where a consistent supply of work for foreign companies exists is in water supply projects. In 1985 a series of contracts was tendered for water treatment and distribution schemes to complement the 13 or so projects bid in 1984. These ranged in value from about $10 million to the $200 million Basra project on which negotiations were begun. The government is proceeding with its plans to expand sewer capacity in the country's major towns. Further work is planned at Basra, and in 1982, further investment in Baghdad's sewer system was estimated at over $1 billion. In 1982, however, consultancy contracts to design second stages for 13 towns were shelved.

The country's electricity network continues to be extended. Power output was put at 11.7 billion kilowatt-hours (kwh) in 1981; by 2000, it is expected to have reached 60 billion kwh. The South Koreans won an order to build a 1,200-megawatt (mw) power station in 1984. At least two more generating plants were planned, one of which may be built by the Soviet Union while the other will probably be delayed. An 800-mw station may be built in the north to feed the Turkish network. Contracts were awarded to supply sections of a massive transmission line as part of the fourth stage of the domestic "supergrid" network. A contract to build four 400-kilovolt (kv) substations is also due to be awarded, and plans have begun on the fifth stage of the grid. A series of awards to build 132-kv substations have been given to Italian, Japanese, French, and Yugoslav firms, and more orders are due to install 132-kv transmission lines. Work has also started on the $427 million second phase of the rural electricity program that will connect more than 3,000 villages to the national grid by 1990. More than 4,000 villages, with about 2 million inhabitants have already been connected. Designs have also been completed to install electricity distribution networks in 10 large towns across the country.

Domestic Priorities, Regional Linkages

The country's emphasis on providing these basic services is a reflection of the leadership's determination to break out of the "third world syndrome," described by Saddam Hussein as "large-scale backwardness, low level of education, with meagre attention paid to development." Thus the planners have tried to couple economic development with social development to build "the new Iraqi character."[17] Such a policy, taken with attempts to decentralize development away from Baghdad, Basra, and Kirkuk, and lately the effort to encourage the private sector, has brought an overall improvement in the life of the Iraqi population and has given the regime a certain degree of popularity. In addition, involvement in the country's economic development has broadened significantly over the last four years as women have emerged to play an important role in Iraq's economy, not only as shop-floor workers or farm laborers but also as designers and engineers. Manpower shortages caused by the demands of the war have accelerated this progress; now mainly women staff Baghdad's offices and it is not unusual to find women project engineers working on-site.

Another high priority for the government has been closer cooperation with Turkey and supportive Arab countries. Baghdad has joint economic and technical cooperation agreements with Turkey, and Saudi Arabia, the United Arab Emirates (UAE), and Qatar among Arab countries. Several of these countries are already providing markets for Iraqi exports of cement, industrial goods, fruit, and vegetables. Iraq has also drawn closer to Saudi Arabia, Turkey, Jordan, and Kuwait because of the political, financial, and economic support each has offered to Iraq. The extensive loans Saudi Arabia and Kuwait have given Iraq were mentioned earlier, and still closer ties are likely once road, rail, and telephone links have been finalized and the trans-Saudi pipeline has been built.

Turkey, Jordan, and Kuwait assumed particularly vital roles when it became impossible to move goods and supplies through the ports of either Iraq or Syria. The Turkish pipeline and the road routes bringing trucks in from Europe probably saved Iraq from near total collapse. There are now plans for Iraq to build a new power station in the north to feed the Turkish national grid, and the two countries' rail networks will also be eventually linked. New oil and gas pipelines between the two countries are planned; Iraq already supplies one-third of Turkey's oil needs. Turkish contractors have also become more bullish in the Iraqi market despite the financial problems.

Before the war started, Iraq had put up several loans to finance projects in Jordan. However, once Baghdad's financial crisis had started to bite Amman quickly turned the tables and offered trade credit. Further Iraqi-Jordanian links will be forged if the problem of security guarantees is solved and an oil pipeline is built to Jordan's Red Sea port of Aqaba. Also in the planning stage is a $1 billion, 1000-kilometer pipeline to supply water to Jordan.

Kuwaiti ports also became indispensable off-loading points for the shipment of military and commercial goods to Iraq. A pipeline project to supply Iraqi water to Kuwait has been discussed for a long while, and road and rail links with Kuwait are planned as well. An oil pipeline from southern Iraq, through Kuwait and the Gulf states to the Indian Ocean, bypassing the Strait of Hormuz has also been discussed, although concrete plans have yet to be formulated.

Beyond these actual and potential bilateral linkages, Iraq has benefitted in recent years from numerous regional associations of both a Gulf-oriented and pan-Arab nature. Assuming the war will allow it, Iraq's land, resources, and people make it an advantageous location to base a variety of regional industrial projects. Although not a member of the Gulf Cooperation Council (GCC), Iraq is a member of the Gulf Organization for Industrial Consulting (GOIC). Nasiriyah will be the site of the country's first GOIC-sponsored project, a $180 million float glass plant, to be run by a pan-Arab company.

The first of the country's large pan-Arab industrial ventures to be set up was a linear alkyl-benzene plant, for which a contract was awarded in 1984. The plant will be run by another Baghdad-based company, the Arab Detergents Chemicals Company (Aradet), in which Iraq and the Arab Petroleum Investments Corporation are the major shareholders. The others are Saudi Arabia's Petromin, Kuwait's Petrochemical Industries Company, and the Amman-based Arab Mining Company. Aradet will be involved in a 50-thousand tons a year sodium tripolyphosphate plant. Another pan-Arab project close to construction start-up is an antibiotics factory to be run by the Baghdad-based Arab Company for Antibiotic Industries.

Other interesting pan-Arab companies based in Baghdad are the Arab Industrial Development Organization (AIDO) and the Arab Industrial Investment Company (AIIC). AIIC plans to set up a 400-thousand tons a year seamless steel pipe factory in Iraq, which will cost up to $1 billion. AIDO and AIIC have acted together on several other projects. In the feasibility stage now are factories to make steel, telephone exchanges, mobile cranes, circuit breakers, and diesel engines. Sites have not yet been selected for these projects, however. Important to Iraq's regional profile, the Baghdad-based AIDO has produced a proposal to build 266 industrial projects throughout the Arab world over the next five years at a total cost of almost $2.5 billion.

Extra-Regional Ties

Outside the Arab world, Baghdad is closely linked with the Soviet Union under the 20-year friendship treaty. Moscow is one of the country's leading suppliers of weapons and in 1984 came forward with funding for oil and power generation projects. Moscow is also closely linked with Iraq's nuclear power program. In 1968, it supplied a 2-mw research reactor and, in 1984, the Soviet company Atomenergoexport was commissioned to identify a site for a planned nuclear power station. (Iraq views nuclear energy as the sole commercially feasible alternative to oil.) Signs show, however, that Baghdad has not been overly impressed with the level of Soviet technology—companies picking up tender documents for an NGL plant have been told that although the plant had been designed by the Soviet Union, it would not be built by Soviet companies. But, under the recent cooperation agreements, Moscow will continue to be involved in Iraq's oil and power generation sectors.

Eastern bloc countries also enjoy close ties as suppliers of food, consumer goods, machinery, industrial plants, and contractors and designers. Technical staff from Poland and Czechoslovakia can be found in such state concerns as the Irrigation Ministry and the State Organization for Roads and Bridges. Many of these countries have cooperation agreements with local universities. State-owned companies from Poland, Czechoslovakia, Romania, and Bulgaria have worked on planning, land reclamation, and industrial projects for many years.

Two countries, Yugoslavia and India, are closely linked as fellow members of the nonaligned movement. In 1984, there were some 16 thousand Yugoslavs working in Iraq for 160 Yugoslav companies, which were estimated to have project work—in both the civil and military sector—worth more than $3 billion. Indian companies have also wanted to maintain and improve their foothold in Iraq and, backed by their government, they have been foremost in bidding for new work over the last year.

A strong West European presence exists in Iraq. West German firms have been represented there since the days of the Baghdad-Berlin railway at the beginning of the twentieth century, and, although now hampered by the lack of financial support, West German contractors, consultants, and plant engineers generally enjoy a good reputation. France and Italy have good relations and, backed by credit made available by their governments, French and Italian companies have picked up oil and power contracts in Iraq over the last year. British consulting engineers are generally well regarded—in Baghdad they are responsible for designing and supervising work on the capital's water and sewer networks. But British contractors have hardly ventured near Iraq.

The war halted a major South Korean incursion into the market, and South Korean companies are now hampered by their lack of financial support. The Chinese have succeeded them as Asia's most competitive contractors. The China State Construction Engineering

Corporation now has some $600 million worth of work in contracts won since the beginning of 1984. Bank of China financing probably backs such work; the bank offered dollar credits at attractive interest rates back in mid-1983. In two 1985 tenders for large dam projects the Chinese emerged as low bidder for both. For one bid, they teamed up with Brazil's Construtora Mendes Junior, which has over $2 billion worth of rail, road, and irrigation schemes under way. The Brazilian company has been promised more work as compensation for extra costs incurred by the war on road and rail contracts.

At the beginning of 1985, Volkswagen do Brasil signed a $630 million deal involving the supply of Brazilian-made cars in exchange for oil. Brazil, which supplies weapons to Iraq, has also made deals for providing food and industrial projects in return for oil.

U.S.-Iraqi Commercial Relations

Since 1983 numerous U.S. firms have competed successfully in Iraq. These include DeLeuw Cather International, Borg-Warner Corporation's York International, Carrier International, NCR International, Mega Tech, and The Architects Collaborative (TAC). Howe-Baker Engineering, General Electric, and Raymond International have also worked there recently. TAC, which has been working on the Baghdad University expansion program since 1958, and Brown & Root have shown it is possible to work continuously in the country despite the problems.

U.S. design firms have been well represented. Apart from TAC, Ventauri Rauch and Scott Brown have designed a large building on Khulafa Street and was asked to submit designs for the state mosque competition. Several other buildings along Khulafa Street in Baghdad have been designed by TAC, which completed the design for a new Sheraton hotel in Mosul. Both the country's other Sheraton hotels (in Basra and Baghdad) were designed by TAC. A new campus for the University of Technology was designed by Perkins & Will, and Jung-Brannen Associates have done a feasibility study for a zoological and botanical garden in Baghdad.

Interest in Iraq among U.S. companies has picked up noticeably since the restoration of U.S.-Iraqi diplomatic relations in 1984. A major trade delegation led by the U.S. Commerce Department completed an important visit to Baghdad in September 1985. It took back to Washington an initialed draft of an Iraqi-U.S. general trade agreement which, upon finalization, would greatly facilitate an expansion of trade relations. Progress was also made during this visit toward an agreement with the U.S. Overseas Private Investment Corporation

(OPIC), which would pave the way for U.S. companies to acquire political risk insurance for work undertaken in Iraq. Furthermore, Iraqi officials held discussions with a visiting senior vice president of the U.S. Export-Import Bank, on requirements for relaxing EXIM Bank credit policies toward Iraq. Visible progress on these fronts would likely lead a larger number of U.S. companies to consider business in Iraq. A private U.S.-Iraq Business Forum has already been established in Washington to facilitate a broader commercial exchange between the two countries.

By way of guidance the Commerce Department has advised U.S. firms that their best prospects are the supply of agricultural commodities, equipment and services, computers and software, food processing equipment, medical apparatus and supplies, irrigation equipment and services, water treatment equipment and services, and petroleum development and exploration equipment and services. It also arranged a water resources mission to Iraq at the beginning of 1984 that discussed business amounting to some $4 billion. In addition, Farouk Salman al-Obaidi, director-general of the Iraqi Trade Ministry's foreign economic relations department, has said that Baghdad is interested in U.S. training programs and technology at all levels, as well as expertise in planning and operating transport activities in ports, airports, roads, and railways.[18]

Conclusion

It is generally assumed that Baghdad is now capable of both sustaining its current level of economic activity and continuing the war as long as it proves necessary. Financing will be necessary for trade and new project work, however. When Ireland extended credit terms to Iraq at the end of 1984, Irish Trade Minister John Bruton said: "I recognize that for the immediate future, the level of exports to Iraq will be influenced to some extent by the availability of export credit insurance cover."[19] Similarly, the UK's two loans have been extended accepting Iraq's short-term difficulties, but recognizing its longer-term economic viability and its past record for financial probity. Iraqi officials clearly believe such optimism is justified, expecting as they do that oil revenues will increase and military expenditures will remain stable. Baghdad's second, albeit more temperate, attempt at guns *and* butter economic policy—hoping in 1986–1990 to make the development progress that eluded it in 1981–1985—should command the continued, close attention of existing and prospective suppliers to this potentially vast market.

A Selected List of Major Projects

In many cases design work has been completed for several of these projects, but implementation has been delayed by the war. The Iraq-Saudi pipeline, phase 2 and the Jordan pipeline are both major projects and covered elsewhere in this volume.

Railways

Baghdad-Basra: More than 900 kilometers of track will link Baghdad with Basra and Umm Qasr ports and eventually with Kuwait and a Gulf network. It is designed by the UK's Henderson Busby Partnership to take passenger trains at a maximum 250 kilometers an hour and freight trains at 120 kilometers an hour. Work will include building two new major stations and 44 medium, small, and wayside stations. The first three stages, Baghdad to Basra via Kut and Nasiriyah, were tendered in 1982. The final contenders for the work, estimated to cost up to $3 billion, were a West German consortium led by Philipp Holzmann and a Brazilian-South Korean joint venture of Construtora Mendes Junior and Hyundai Engineering & Construction Company. No decision was reached and the project is unlikely to go ahead while the war continues. The client for this and all new railway construction work is the New Railways Implementation Authority.

Baghdad to Mosul, via Kirkuk and Arbil: A French team led by Sofrerail has completed detailed design work and tender documents were prepared for some 600 kilometers of track. Work is not likely to go ahead, although if Turkey decides that the Iraqi link with its own network should take place, then government may decide to tender the Kirkuk-Mosul section and a 100-kilometer section between Mosul to Zakho on the Turkish border. Designs for this last section have been completed by Henderson Busby Partnership.

Baghdad loop line: All proposed lines into Baghdad will connect with a 112-kilometer loop around the capital, designed by Italy's Sotecni. Work will also include alterations to the capital's two main railway stations and setting up a large freight marshalling yard.

Automobile

Car assembly plant: The status of this project is unclear because of its estimated cost of more than $3 billion. Design work has been completed by a West German team led by Weidleplan, however. Initial proposals were for a plant, with electronically controlled production lines, to produce 150 thousand saloon cars, 25 thousand trucks, and 15 thousand tractors. Development would also include factories to produce gear boxes, engines, tires, batteries, paints, and metal and plastic components. It was expected to employ 20 thousand people, and a new town was envisaged, at a cost of more than $2 billion, for the workers and their families.

New Towns

To cope with projected increase to 12 million in Baghdad's population before 2000, at least three new towns will be built within a 100–120 kilometer radius of the capital. The first is at Tharthar, for 100 thousand people by 1990 and 150 thousand by 2000. A master plan is being made by Greece's Doxiadis Associates. The other two are similar—the largest will be at Suwayra, about 60 kilometers southeast of Baghdad, for 350 thousand people by 2000. Its master plan is expected from the UK's Shankland Cox. The client, the New Towns Commission, will probably plan the third town—for 80 thousand people—at Madain. The master plan update and development plan for the capital—Baghdad 2001, the Integrated Capital Development Plan—is being done by a group of Japanese consultants called the Japanese Consortium of Consulting Firms (JCCF).

Sewers

Baghdad has been the focus of most of the country's major sewer development work. It is difficult to estimate how much extra work has been let under existing contracts, but in mid-1981, future investment was estimated at $1.3 billion and included main and subsidiary sewers, pumping stations, and extensions to treatment plants. The main consultant for sewerage work in the capital is the UK's Haiste International. The development of second-stage sewer expansion is also planned for Kirkuk, Sulaimaniyah, Arbil, Al Hindiyah, Hit, Zubayr, Diwaniyah, Samawa, Nasiriyah, Ramadi, Al Hillah, Al Kut, and Kerbala. West Germany's Beller Consult has completed designs for the third phase of the Basra sewer scheme, which will involve extending the treatment plant to serve an additional 600 thousand people.

Airports

Mosul International Airport: The design and tender documents have been completed by West German consultant Weidleplan.

Arbil airport: Smaller than Mosul, Arbil with its 3,000-meter runway will be mainly for regional traffic. A consortium of UK consultants led by Scott Wilson Kirkpatrick & Partners completed the designs and tender documents. Regional airports have also been planned for Najaf, Kirkuk, and Amara.

Roads

Expressway Number 2 is still under design by Denmark's Cowi-consult. The 525-kilometer expressway, at an estimated cost of about $3.3 billion, is intended to link Baghdad with the Turkish border town of Zakho via Samara, Kirkuk, Arbil, Mosul, and Dohuk.

Expressway Number 3, still in an early stage, is planned as an alternative route to Basra via Al Kut and Amara.

According to a master plan for road developments in Baghdad, a considerable amount of work remains in the capital, including new expressway routes, extensions to existing ones, several more bridges across the Tigris, and three or four road tunnels under the river.

The Baghdad Metro

Costs are estimated at up to $10 billion. The general consultant is a consortium of UK companies called British Metro Consultants Group (BMCG). To date, two detailed design contracts remain to be let. DeLeuw Cather International is working on detailed designs for one section of track, assisted by Karn Charuhas Chapman & Twohey (KCCT). The first stage will comprise 32 kilometers of line, with 36 stations, to be extended after 1990 to take a 1 million passengers per day capacity. Civil works contractors still need to be prequalified; a second round of prequalification is likely for mechanical and electrical suppliers.

Universities

At least three new campuses are planned as well as continuing expansion of existing universities at Baghdad, Basra, and Mosul.

Rashid University, now under design by West German consultant Heinle, Wischer & Partner, was intended to take initially 14,500 students. The university will include agriculture, veterinary, and medical faculties, as well as 25-thousand-seat stadium and a 450-bed hospital. The site is 35 kilometers southeast of Baghdad.

Salahaddin University is to be built in Arbil at an estimated construction cost of $1 billion. Designed by a consortium led by France's SCET International for 12–16 thousand students, it will have four main faculties—engineering, medicine, arts, and science.

The new campus for Baghdad's University of Technology was designed and its tender documents have been completed by U.S. consultant Perkins & Will International. The new campus, to be built

TABLE 1. Iraqi Trade Figures, 1982–1984
        Imports from and Exports to Selected Countries
        (In Millions of U.S. Dollars)

Country	IMPORTS			EXPORTS		
	1982	1983	1984	1982	1983	1984
Brazil	319	416	224	2,573	2,071	1,369
France	1,433	809	685	2,666	496	787
Italy	1,530	738	600	1,420	1,112	1,000
Japan	2,757	632	677	777	141	270
Soviet Union	—	476	318	—	490	779
Turkey	610	820	934	1,470	947	943
United Kingdom	1,529	608	459	139	48	92
United States	846	512	664	42	61	124
West Germany	3,143	1,467	861	229	393	477
Yugoslavia	—	—	306	—	—	380

Source: Middle East Economic Digest.

about 10 kilometers from the center of Baghdad, will be for about 16 thousand students.

Baghdad University expansion includes the building of four faculties, staff housing, a 205-thousand-seat stadium, and a large auditorium. The Architects Collaborative of the United States has been working on this 12-stage program since 1958.

Notes

1. President Saddam Hussein, *Baghdad Observer*, July 17, 1985.

2. *Middle East Times*, August 25, 1985.

3. Deputy Premier and Foreign Affairs Minister Tariq Aziz, press conference, July 1983 in Baghdad, reported in *Middle East Economic Digest (MEED)*, July 22, 1983, p. 22.

4. Tariq Aziz, press conference, November 1984 in Washington, D.C., reported in *MEED*, December 7, 1984, p. 19.

5. Oil Minister Qassem Ahmad Taqi, interview reported in *Middle East Economic Survey*, May 20, 1985, p. A2–A5.

6. Ibid.

7. Tariq Aziz, press conference, July 1983 in Baghdad, reported in *MEED*, July 22, 1983.

8. First Deputy Premier Taha Yassin Ramadan, *Baghdad Observer*, October 24, 1984, p. 4.

9. Taha Yassin Ramadan, January 1984 in Baghdad, reported in *MEED*, January 13, 1984, p. 14.

10. Central Political Report of the Arab Ba'th Socialist Party's 9th Regional Congress, June 1983, translation by Naji al-Hadithi, part 4, *Baghdad Observer,* May 2, 1984.

11. Ibid.

12. Taha Yassin Ramadan, May 1984 at Mosul University, reported in *Baghdad Observer,* May 15, 1984.

13. "Private Sector: Indispensable in National Development," *Baghdad Observer,* September 25, 1984.

14. "Bright Future for Private Industrialists," *Baghdad Observer,* January 1, 1985.

15. President Saddam Hussein, speech to industrialists, August 14, 1984 in Baghdad, reported in *MEED,* August 17, 1984, p. 11.

16. Taha Yassin Ramadan, in a speech reported in *Baghdad Observer,* July 30, 1984.

17. Saddam Hussein, news conference, July 1981 in Baghdad, reported in *MEED,* August 7, 1981, p. 25.

18. See excerpts of Dr. Obaidi's remarks in "The U.S. and Iraq: Marking a New Phase in Political and Trade Relations," in *U.S.-Arab Commerce,* May 1985, pp. 18–20.

19. Ireland's Industry, Trade and Commerce Minister John Bruton, Dublin, November 27, 1984, *MEED,* December 7, 1984, p. 16.

4

Iraq in the Gulf

Edmund Ghareeb

An article published a few years ago in the London *Economist* reveals the misunderstanding and bafflement that permeate much of Western writing about Iraq and its policies. It stated, "Iraq is the country that breaks all the rules. Long the Soviet Union's satellite in the Middle East, it is spinning away just as the Russians begin to take a close interest in the region. Long the oddball of Arabia, it has taken on in the name of all Arabs, a Persian giant others have long feared. Long Islam's most ardent revolutionary, it has gone to war with Islam's newest revolution. Long the subverter of conservative Arab regimes, its two closest friends at the moment are Jordan, ruled by the cousin of the Hashemite royal family murdered during Iraq's grim first chapter of revolution, and Saudi Arabia, the plutocratic Midas of the Arab world."[1]

This article in the *Economist* and other more recent articles in the American media show that Iraq has been and to a large extent remains one of the more stereotyped and least understood countries in the Arab-Persian Gulf region, and perhaps in the Arab world. On one hand, Iraq's actions are frequently portrayed simply as the manifestations of a secretive, xenophobic, violent, and authoritarian society. On the other hand, its role in and policy toward the Gulf area have generally been ignored in the rather large body of recent literature on the economic, political, and security issues affecting the Gulf states. Despite its oil wealth, geographic position, substantial agricultural and industrial potential, and its large water resources, seldom has Iraq been dealt with as a littoral state with legitimate interests of its own in the Gulf. Even today, the Iran-Iraq war is often viewed only in terms of its impact and possible spillover in the other Gulf states. Nevertheless, while Iraq lacked until recently the means to become closely involved in Gulf affairs, the definition of its Gulf policy has been sharpened by its history, geographic position, economic and security interests, and now Ba'thist ideology.

59

To begin to understand Iraq's foreign policy objectives, including its policy toward the Gulf, however, it is essential to keep in mind Iraq's special circumstances in the Arab world. Iraq is the largest Arab country in the Gulf in terms of population, military forces, and human resource capabilities, and the most committed to Arab nationalism as an ideology. Furthermore, Iraq—as Iraqis never tire of repeating—has been the cradle of mankind's most ancient civilizations and the hub of some of the world's greatest empires and centers of learning. Iraq has enjoyed strength and prosperity; it has also suffered under invasions, occupation, tyranny, poverty, and backwardness. In this light, one can appreciate statements by Iraqi leaders about the need to repeat the historic role "played by our ancestors in the service of the Arab nation and humanity."[2]

Iraq's geographic position on the frontier between the Arab and non-Arab worlds has led both Iraqi and non-Iraqi Arabs to look at Iraq as the guardian of the Eastern gate of the Arab world. In addition to sharing borders with the Arab countries of Jordan, Syria, Saudi Arabia, and Kuwait, Iraq shares frontiers with two large Muslim but non-Arab countries, Iran and Turkey, both of which occupied Iraq in the recent past. It is also closer than many other Arab states to non-Arab and even non-Muslim peoples in the East. Thus, none of the other Arab states, including those bordering non-Arab peoples, face the cultural, political, or military challenges faced by Iraq. The nature of the Iraqi perception of this challenge helps to explain the constant emphasis by Iraqi leaders on the need to protect the independence and Arab identity of Iraq and of the "Arab character of the Gulf."

Pre-1958 Policy

This Arab character of the Gulf position on the part of Iraq's leadership has usually been explained by Western observers either in terms of Iraq's desire for hegemony in the Gulf or of Ba'thist ideology, which emphasizes Arab unity as an essential solution to the region's problems.[3] Iraqi concern for the Arab-ness of the Gulf, however, was manifested as early as the 1930s in, for example, newspaper editorials lambasting the Iraqi government for failing to respond to the calls for closer cooperation between the Gulf emirates and Iraq. Warnings were issued about the "numerous foreign elements who are constantly competing with the local population in these Arab lands" and who harbor "wide-ranging and secret political designs" against the emirates.[4] Emphasis was also placed on Iraq's need to establish close economic ties with each of the Arab emirates having "national and religious ties with Iraq," and to open consulates in Bahrain and Kuwait.[5] Under King Ghazi, some Iraqi parties issued halfhearted calls for uniting Kuwait with Iraq. These calls and attempts at closer Iraqi-Kuwaiti interaction were not welcomed by the British, who acted to discourage such moves.[6]

Such Iraqi notions about Kuwait were based on the fact that Kuwait had once been part of the *wilaya* (or administrative district) of Basra during the Ottoman period. Iraq supplied Kuwait with grain, fruit, vegetables, and fresh water transported by boat from the Shatt al-Arab, and Kuwaiti ships plied southern Iraq. The sheikh of Kuwait owned date plantations in the vicinity of Basra, and when, during the 1930s, the government of Iraq began encouraging nationalism in the Gulf, it was with special attention to Kuwait.

Nevertheless, Iraq's practical involvement in Gulf affairs prior to 1958 was limited. Before then, economic, political, and strategic factors directed the country's attention away from the south and toward Syria, Iran, and Turkey. During the tenure of the Hashemite monarchy, the Gulf was controlled by Great Britain, which effectively prevented Iraq from asserting any interest in the area. Second, rivalry between the Saudis and the Hashemites, as well as King Faisal's hopes of uniting the countries of the Fertile Crescent, attracted Iraqi attention to the north. Third, Iraq lacked the military and economic means to influence Gulf affairs at that time. Its geography, economy, and political interests favored the development of close ties with Turkey, Iran, and the Fertile Crescent, and later (in 1956–1957) Saudi Arabia.

Iraq's foreign policy has also been strongly affected by the competing pressures of its diverse ethnic and religious groups. The problems arising from its mosaic-like human landscape, unmatched by any other Arab country, are attested to in a secret memorandum submitted by Iraq's first king, King Faisal, to some of his closest aides:

> Iraq is one of those countries which lack the most important force necessary for social cohesion. This government rules over a Kurdish group which includes persons with personal ambitions who call upon this group to abandon the government because it is not of this race. (It also) rules a Shi'a plurality which belongs to the same ethnic group as the government but as a result of the discrimination which the Shi'is incurred under Ottoman rule which did not allow them to participate in the affairs of government, a wide breach developed between the two sects . . . I discussed these great masses of people without mentioning the other minorities, including Christians, which were encouraged to demand different rights . . . I say with my heart full of sadness that there is not yet in Iraq an Iraqi people.[7]

The complex of tribal, intellectual, and sectarian differences referred to in this memorandum plagued the very future of the Iraqi state itself. Arab nationalists argued that the state was an artificial creation by Britain to serve its own interests and that the only natural structure would be a larger, unified Arab state in which Iraq would play the role of the Arab Prussia.[8] Others in Iraq, however, favored the perpetuation of an independent Iraq, fearing internal conflict, possible secession, or territorial rearrangements because of potential Shi'a and Kurdish opposition to Arab unity.[9]

Under the monarchy, foreign policy was largely shaped by Nuri al-Said following King Faisal's death. It aimed primarily at preserving Iraqi independence and territorial integrity and at uniting the Fertile Crescent under Hashemite rule (King Faisal had also been king of Syria for two years), while maintaining close and friendly relations with Turkey and Iran and later with Saudi Arabia. This policy, which appeared to have been successful before World War II, began to come apart after the war. Nuri sought an end to the security treaties with Britain because of anxiety over the rising influence of Arab nationalism as a radical ideology and of the Iraqi Communist Party (ICP), but he accepted U.S. Secretary of State John Foster Dulles' proposal of an alliance of the northern tier states to contain Soviet influence in the Gulf (later known as the Baghdad Pact). His Arab Union with Jordan further alienated Iraq from the Nasser-led Arab nationalists and the Ba'th, who favored non-involvement in the Cold War and saw the Arab Union as a deterrent to Arab unity. This alienation was an important factor in the decline of the monarchy and its overthrow in July 1958.

Post-1958 Policy

The overthrow of the monarchy and the accession to power of Abd al-Karim Qasim led to a number of changes in foreign policy. Iraq withdrew from the Baghdad Pact, abrogated its 1954 military agreement with Britain, and resumed diplomatic relations with the Soviet Union. Also following the 1958 revolution there was a growing importance of the Gulf in Iraqi affairs. The new government faced serious economic difficulties when it sought to improve living standards and increase military capability. As a result, it turned to the foreign-owned Iraq Petroleum Company (IPC) for increased revenues.[10] For political as well as economic reasons, IPC refused to accede to demands for increased production and a share of the profits on each barrel produced.

Although government pressure failed to get the IPC to allow it a share in the operation of the company, it nevertheless forced the company to promise to double its production in 1962. This development forced the oil companies to build new handling, transport, loading, and storage facilities—mostly in the south in order to avoid interruptions similar to the Syrian one in 1956. The Qasim government tried to advance commercial activity in the south. Work started on a rail line connecting Baghdad and Basra, bidding opened for the reconstruction of new port at Um Qasr on the Gulf, funds were allocated for the expansion of the port of Basra, and a modest shipping company was established to conduct foreign trade.

Another indication of the regime's growing interest in Gulf affairs was the Qasim government's attempt to gain sovereignty over Kuwait in 1961. The Iraqi-Kuwaiti crisis developed after Kuwait gained independence after June 19, 1961. On June 25, Qasim declared that Kuwait, "arbitrarily held by imperialism," belonged to Iraq.[11] The Kuwaiti government declared a state of emergency and placed its armed forces on alert. Both Arab and British pressure prevented Qasim from carrying through his threats of annexing Kuwait. This episode had two effects. It ultimately spurred Iraq to take a greater interest in the Gulf states. It also reinforced Iraq's image in the West as a "radical expansionist threat" to the other states of the Gulf. The sudden interest in the Gulf, however, had a significant impact on the economy of southern Iraq, directly influencing the policy of the Ba'th government that took power in 1968.

During the regimes of Abd al-Salam Arif (1963–1966) and Abd al-Rahman Arif (1966–1968), Iraq began to show a desire to play a greater role in the region, despite the constraints caused by the continued British presence there. Under the first Ba'th regime in 1963, Qasim's historical claim to Kuwait was abandoned, and an Iraqi-Kuwaiti rapprochement became possible. Economic relations between the two countries improved, as trade increased and Kuwaiti public and private investments poured into Iraq. On the political and diplomatic scene, Kuwait supported Iraqi attempts to persuade the countries of the lower Gulf to abandon British protection. Additionally, ties between Iraq and the lower Gulf emirates grew during this period. Iraq was one of the first states to welcome the proposal to form a federation of the conservative emirates of the lower Gulf, because such a move would hasten British withdrawal from the area. Relations with Saudi Arabia remained somewhat tense and insubstantial. These relations were complicated by the conflict in Yemen, in which Iraq backed the Republican government, and Saudi Arabia supported the

Royalist insurgents. Arif's pursuit of a "unified political command" with Egypt further strained Iraq's relations with Saudi Arabia.

The Ba'th Return to Power

Active Iraqi involvement in the Gulf did not emerge, however, until after the Ba'th party returned to power in the bloodless July 17–30 Revolution of 1968. Unlike coups staged in the 1960s by military officers in many Arab and Third World countries, the 1968 Ba'thist takeover of Iraq was a revolutionary effort backed by an ideological party with concrete programs and goals and members whose commitment to Ba'thist ideology had been tested by many years of underground activity and struggle.[12]

During their first two to three years in power, the Ba'thists were preoccupied with warding off plots against the regime and with preserving their authority. It soon became clear that under no circumstances were they prepared to allow political opponents to conspire against the regime or to tolerate less threatening opposition prior to consolidating their authority. In foreign policy the party was primarily concerned with following an independent and nonaligned foreign policy and with ending all traces of foreign control over various parts of the "Arab homeland" through protracted struggle against imperialism, Zionism, and Arab reaction.

In addition, one of the main characteristics of Iraq's foreign policy under the Ba'thists was the shift from seeking a leadership role in the Fertile Crescent area to seeking one in the Gulf. This trend was influenced by five external factors. The first was Britain's declaration of its intention to withdraw from the Gulf. The Ba'thists believed that this action was going to affect the future of the power structure in the area and was going to lead to the "tightening of imperialist, political, economic and military control of the area."[13] The second factor was the decline of Nasserist influence in the Gulf following the 1967 war, which left the field open for the Ba'thists to carry the mantle of pan-Arabism and to cooperate with other nationalist and radical forces in the Gulf. The third related to the growing importance of oil, particularly after the energy crisis and oil embargo of 1973. Oil in the area ceased to be merely a target for foreign investment, but also became a matter of great strategic importance. Lines of transportation and communication became as important as the oil itself. The fourth factor was the bitter feud between the Syrian and Iraqi Ba'thists that greatly limited Iraqi efforts to project its influence into the Fertile Crescent area. The fifth was the Iraqi leaders' growing concern about the security and survival of their regime in an area dominated by conservative opponents. U.S. efforts to get Iran to police the Gulf following the British withdrawal were seen as an attempt

- to change the Arab character of the Gulf by encouraging non-Arab (Iranian) immigration to the Arab countries,
- to promote outside control of the area and its natural resources,
- to isolate and if possible liquidate the Iraqi and South Yemeni regimes in order to strike at the Arab revolutionary movement inside and outside the Gulf, and
- to impose a U.S. solution on the Arab-Israeli conflict.[14]

In addition to these external factors, Iraq's interest in the Gulf was enhanced by several domestic economic and political concerns. In its search for stability, the government was aware of the need to improve the living standards of its people by diversifying Iraq's sources of revenues and by promoting its vast industrial and agricultural potential. In order to achieve these objectives, the government needed new revenues and could only increase its revenues quickly through its substantial oil wealth. Thus, the major goal of the government became the nationalization of oil, which had long been the aim of the Ba'thists.

By 1970, the failure of the IPC to increase oil production had come to be viewed by the government as an effort "to contain the revolution by delaying tactics to gain its downfall."[15] When the IPC finally refused to negotiate after it was given a two week ultimatum by the government in May 1972, Iraq nationalized the northern oilfields, which accounted for about 65 percent of the total oil produced in Iraq. The Iraqi government decided, however, that it was not in Iraq's national interest to nationalize all of the IPC's oil holdings, because the government could not operate all the oil fields and it needed the currency paid by the company. For this reason and also because of Iraq's flourishing economic cooperation with France, the French partner of the IPC was allowed to continue to receive its share of oil under the same schedule for the next 10 years.

Iraq had been prepared for this confrontation with the IPC, as just one month earlier, in April 1972, it had signed a 15-year treaty of friendship with the Soviet Union. Confronted by hostility from its neighbors and by a Kurdish rebellion at home, Iraq needed to show that it was not isolated or friendless. Also it needed Soviet technical and economic aid for political development and backing during the nationalization of the IPC and Soviet arms and political support in dealing with the Kurdish opposition and the Iraqi Communist Party.

The nationalization of oil and the increased revenues it furnished had a dramatic impact on Iraq's economy and spurred major infrastructural developments that helped change its approach to the Gulf. These included increased construction of oil industry facilities, particularly in the southern area bordering the Gulf; construction of a new strategic pipeline linking the pumping station at Haditha with Turkey and with the new offshore oil terminal at Mina al-Bakr; large investments in port facilities; and a national tanker fleet and development of Iraq's industrial and commercial capabilities.[16] Iraq's growing economy also implied the greater strategic significance of the Gulf. Iraq is confined to 38 miles of coastline on the Gulf and shallow-water ports. Consequently, its economic security became vulnerable to the increasing power of neighboring Gulf states, particularly Iran. As a result of its growing economic and strategic interests in the Gulf, Iraq was led to assert its claim to the Kuwaiti islands of Warba and Bubyan, which dominate the estuary on which Iraq's new port of Um Qasr is located. Hence, the Gulf became a major factor in Iraq's foreign policy for ideological, economic, and strategic reasons.

The Phases of Ba'thist Gulf Policy

Broadly speaking, Ba'thist Iraq's foreign policy toward the Gulf has passed through four distinct and clearly identifiable phases. The first phase extended from 1968 to 1970 and was characterized by a policy of nationalist and ideological confrontation with Iran and by attempts to forge closer ties with the Arab states of the Gulf. The second lasted roughly from 1970 to 1975 and was primarily a period of ideological confrontation with both Iran and with its Arab neighbors. In the third phase, from about 1975 to 1979, Iraq followed a policy of rapprochement and détente on the basis of noninterference in the internal affairs of its neighboring states. From 1979 to the present, Iraq has followed a policy of cooperation with its Arab neighbors and one of confrontation with the new regime in Tehran.

During the first phase, Iraq was unable to play a major role in expanding its ideology to the Gulf, in preventing Iran from posing as the Gulf strongman, and in inducing the other Arab states to join it in a common stand against Tehran. Between 1968 and 1970, Iraq appealed to the Arab Gulf states to join it in a united front in defense of Arab interests in Palestine and the Gulf and for the nationalization of oil resources. Iraq supported the creation of a federation among the seven emirates and Qatar and Bahrain as "a fence protecting the Gulf from imperialism,"[17] and also tried, without much success, to check Iran's growing role in the Gulf by cooperating with Saudi

Arabia. Iraq hoped to build on the strained relations between Iran and Saudi Arabia over the shah's claims to Bahrain. The Ba'thist regime prompted the two monarchies to move closer together, however, by its advocacy of a radical ideology and its commitment to radical social and economic change. When Iraq proposed a military agreement with Saudi Arabia in May 1969, during a visit by the Saudi Foreign Minister to Baghdad, it was rejected. Baghdad also failed to win Saudi support in its confrontation with Iran following the latter's abrogation of the Shatt al-Arab treaty in 1969.

In 1970 U.S. Undersecretary of State Elliott Richardson invoked the Nixon Doctrine of reliance on regional allies to defend regional security during a visit to Tehran, and he hinted that Iran might play the role of the guardian of Gulf security. The exchange of visits between the Saudi foreign minister who traveled to Tehran in April 1970 and the return visit by the Iranian foreign minister amidst talk of a U.S.-backed security arrangement served to intensify Iraqi suspicions and feelings of isolation and encirclement.

These developments led Iraq to reassess its approach to the Gulf and to follow a policy of ideological confrontation with both Iran and the neighboring Arab states, and to seek support from the Soviet Union. Relations between Iraq and the conservative Arab Gulf states, including Saudi Arabia, further polarized with increased Soviet-Iraqi cooperation, beginning in 1970, as well as with Iraq's backing for the Dhofar Liberation Front in Oman and its support of the People's Democratic Republic of Yemen. In the meantime, Saudi Arabia, with U.S. government encouragement, began a major arms buildup, announcing that it would spend billions of dollars on modernizing its armed forces.

Relations between Saudi Arabia and the other Arab Gulf states and Iraq deteriorated further as Iraq advanced its claim on Kuwait's Warba and Bubyan islands. The situation began to deteriorate in 1969 when Kuwait acquiesced under pressure to Iraqi demands that Iraqi troops be stationed on Kuwait's side of the border between Warba and Bubyan in order to protect the Iraqi port of Um Qasr from possible Iranian attack following the renewal of the Shatt al-Arab dispute. Determined to demonstrate its intent to play a role in the region, Iraq attempted to enforce her garrison at Um Qasr and one month later demanded that Kuwait either surrender or lease to Iraq the two islands. When the Kuwaitis rejected the Iraqi demand, minor clashes ensued. Following Arab pressures and mediation attempts, Iraq agreed to withdraw its troops, but stated that the matter was one of direct negotiation between the two countries.

The hostility and suspicion in its relations with Iran were clearly the critical aspect of Iraq's Gulf policy from 1968–1975. The dispute pitted a conservative, non-Arab monarchy whose ruler was seeking to preserve his throne, play a dominant role in Gulf affairs, and assume a prominent international posture against an Arab nationalist and socialist regime aiming at maintaining itself in power, spreading its ideology to other Arab regions, and thwarting Iran's aims in the Gulf. Iran viewed with intense suspicion the socialist and Arab nationalist regime that advocated the preservation of Gulf Arabism and the rejection of security arrangements dominated by Iran, while the Ba'thists spoke of the existence of a deliberate plan by Zionism and imperialism (with Iran as a third partner) to fragment the Arab homeland. Moreover, Iraq viewed the Iranian immigration to the Gulf countries as a part of a systematic plan sponsored by the shah to alter the Arab character of the Gulf. Ba'thist aspirations ran directly counter to the shah's goal "to regain our historic and natural position in the Persian Gulf."[18]

Hostility surfaced early and was sustained through most of this period, beginning with Iranian collusion in a conspiracy to overthrow the Ba'thist regime in February 1969. In April 1969, Iraq decided to enforce its territorial right in Shatt al-Arab under a 1937 treaty and required Iranian ships to pay entry tolls to the Iraqi port authority. Iran refused and began to send naval units to accompany its ships, and then on April 19 unilaterally abrogated the 1937 treaty, claiming that it had been imposed on Iran by the British. Iraq retaliated by expelling thousands of Iranians living in Iraq, boycotting Iranian goods, and giving asylum to leftist and religious opponents of the shah. In addition, support was given to groups calling for self rule in Khuzistan (Arabistan), Kurdistan, and Baluchistan. These and other tensions were reflected in a number of initiatives that Iraq took between 1970 and 1972 to increase the security of the regime. These actions included:

1. The March 11, 1970 Manifesto, which offered autonomy to the Kurds and a peaceful solution to the Kurdish rebellion, and enhanced Iraq's rapport with the Soviet Union, which had been urging a negotiated settlement of this thorny problem;

2. The consolidation of power through the demotion or ouster of leading Ba'thist military figures, which concentrated power in the hands of the civilian wing of the party led by Saddam Hussein and backed by then-President General Ahmad Hasan al-Bakr;

3. Proclamation of the 1971 National Action Charter, which brought the Communist and Kurdish opposition, as well as independent figures, into participation in the political process with the Ba'th Party;

4. Conclusion of a 15-year treaty of friendship with the Soviet Union and consolidation of Iraqi ties with the socialist bloc; and

5. Nationalization of the IPC, which laid the foundation of economic independence.

The primary outlet for Iranian-Iraqi hostility was the Kurdish rebellion in Iraq, which offered the shah a formidable opportunity to destabilize or overthrow the Ba'thist government in Baghdad.[19] The shah, Israel, and the United States (secretly) all offered military and economic aid to the long-time leader of the Kurds, Mullah Mustafa al-Barzani. Encouraged by promises of aid from three countries, the Kurdish leader Barzani escalated his demands for Kurdish autonomy from the central government. The Ba'thist regime, at times backed by the Soviets, made several attempts to reach an agreement with Barzani. But when in March of 1974 these efforts failed because of Kurdish-Ba'thist differences over the terms of autonomy and because of external meddling, Iraq unilaterally implemented the March 11 Manifesto in the Kurdish areas under its control. In heavy fighting throughout 1974 and early 1975, the Iraqi armed forces made costly but steady advances against the Kurdish forces. When Iran, which had escalated its aid to the Kurdish forces, was confronted with increasing its military aid and possibly escalating its intervention and becoming involved in direct or indirect war with Iraq, it opted instead for accommodation with Iraq.

As a result, in March 1975 the shah and Saddam Hussein concluded the Algiers accord. Iraq conceded Iranian claims along the Shatt al-Arab and ended its support for Iranian opponents of the shah. In exchange, Iranian, U.S., and Israeli aid to Mullah Mustafa al-Barzani's Kurdish movement was ended and some 400 square kilometers of land along the border was to be returned to Iraqi sovereignty. Both sides also agreed to end interference in each other's internal affairs, a major source of tension between the two countries.

The Calm before the Storm

The third phase of Ba'thist Iraq's policy in the Gulf lasted from 1974/1975 to 1979, and in it Iraq pursued rapprochement and détente with both its Arab and Iranian neighbors. Iraq's efforts to improve ties with the Arab Gulf states preceded the signing of the 1975 Algiers accord with Iran. In an attempt to enhance ties with the Gulf states and to improve its position vis-à-vis Iran, a small Iraqi naval force visited Saudi, Qatari, Bahraini and Kuwaiti ports, and its commander called for a joint naval force to protect Arab interests.[20] Talks were held with Saudi officials on the topic and the Iraqi foreign minister repeated the suggestion during a visit by Saudi officials to Baghdad in June 1975.

Saudi Arabia for its part was becoming increasingly concerned over Iran's role in the Gulf and her interference in the internal affairs of some Arab states, particularly the stationing of Iranian troops in Oman. It was also interested in reducing Iraq's reliance on the Soviet Union. The shift in Baghdad's policy was reflected in its dealings with Saudi Arabia and during the 1974 Rabat summit when Sheikh Zayed bin Sultan al-Nahyan, the president of the United Arab Emirates, sought to improve Saudi-Iraqi ties. During a discussion of the issue Saddam Hussein told Sheikh Zayed that he did not hold "anything specific" against Saudi Arabia and that he was ready to exchange visits with the Saudis and to reach an understanding with them.[21] The Saudis expressed readiness to improve ties with Iraq and work toward a common Arab policy if Iraq was prepared to resolve a number of bilateral issues, such as frontier delineations, the neutral zone, tribal migration, and smuggling. The Iraqis agreed and visits were exchanged between high-ranking officials.

The atmosphere was further improved by the Iraqi-Iranian Algiers accord, which was concluded during an OPEC conference in March 1975. Saudi Prince Fahd, who was representing King Faisal, welcomed the accord and announced that he would visit Baghdad in April.[22] By signing, Iraq showed that it could work with the more conservative monarchical regimes in the Gulf. The agreement pleased the Saudis because they perceived it as weakening Soviet influence in the Gulf and would end Iraqi support for radical groups in the Gulf region.

Saudi determination to play a more active foreign policy role may have also contributed to improving ties with Iraq. While Prince Fahd's visit was delayed by King Faisal's death, the director-general of the border police visited Baghdad in April 1975, where he reached an agreement with the Iraqis on the division of the neutral zone between the two countries. Fahd's visit came shortly after the signing of the agreement. Furthermore, Saudi Arabia sought to mediate Iraqi disputes with Syria and Kuwait. For example, Petroleum Minister Zaki Yamani sought to resolve the Euphrates water dispute in the spring of 1975, but without great success. Finally, Saudi Arabia also agreed to loan Iraq $200 million.[23]

Improvement in Iraqi-Gulf ties was reflected in Iraq's May 1975 invitation to the chiefs of staff of the smaller Gulf states to attend Iraqi military maneuvers and discuss Gulf security issues. This pattern was continued during a goodwill visit by Revolutionary Command Council member and Iraqi Interior Minister Izzat al-Duri to the Gulf states in April 1977. Al-Duri had previously visited Saudi Arabia, met with his counterpart Prince Nayif, and signed a border agreement that Nayif stated would lead to "positive results" for the security of the two countries. The agreement is reported to have dealt with border control, tribal migration, smuggling, exchange of criminals, and other technical and administrative matters.[24] The Iraqis also began to focus more on the area of economic cooperation with the Gulf states. Moreover, Iraq and Saudi Arabia affirmed their interest in joint economic, technical, and trade cooperation during an Arab Trade Ministers conference in October 1977.

Disagreement remained, however, over oil policies and attempts to isolate Iraq from a security system involving Saudi Arabia and the smaller Gulf states. Iraq and Iran criticized Saudi oil policies when the Saudis decided to raise oil prices by only 5 percent in 1976.[25] Meanwhile, Saudi Arabia and the Gulf states rejected overtures by Iraq for joint cooperation on regional defense. Instead they appeared to be moving on their own in the direction of maintaining the "security and stability of the region and the progress of its peoples and to keep the area outside the spheres of foreign influence."[26]

Relations between Iraq and the other Gulf states further improved following President Sadat's visit to Jerusalem and the Camp David accords. Iraq appeared to be following a policy of coalition building in the Arab world. The occurrence of these two events helped Iraq to smooth its relations with its Arab neighbors. Following the signing of the accords, Iraq succeeded in achieving two regional reconciliations, one with the Gulf states and the other with Syria, vis-à-vis the Arab-Israeli conflict. The rapprochement with the Syrians did not last, however, because of a resurgence of deep-seated intra-Ba'th party rivalries.

Iraq modified some of its previous radical positions to improve ties with the Saudis and other moderate states during the Baghdad summit conference. On the resolution adopted on Egypt, Iraq agreed not to push for sanctions unless Egypt formally signed a peace treaty with Israel. Iraq also signed the joint communique calling for "a just peace based on total Israeli withdrawal" from the Arab territories occupied in 1967. This was the first instance of Iraq indicating acceptance of a peaceful settlement with Israel. Its previous policy had been to reject UN Resolution 242 and to reject alliance with

Arab states that accepted it. Iraq further refrained from pushing for a tough line to punish Egypt following its signing of the Camp David accords during the 1979 Tunis summit in order to avoid embarrassing the conservative Gulf states.

The overthrow of the shah and the nature of the U.S. response had an impact on the Gulf states that led to broad disenchantment with U.S. policy.[27] Iraq, for its part, sought to improve its image as a moderating force in the Arabian peninsula by seeking to resolve the dispute between North and South Yemen. The Iraqis appear to have been motivated by a desire to gain the confidence of Saudi Arabia and other Gulf countries, to allay the Saudi kingdom's security concerns, and to discourage stronger military ties between Saudi Arabia and the United States. Also of concern was the need to strengthen the Iraqi-led coalition that had emerged during the Baghdad summit.[28]

Iraq also appeared to move closer to the Saudi position by strengthening North Yemen through economic and military aid. Iraq offered to train Yemen's military and provided $30 million in economic support.[29] Iraq's critical response to the Soviet invasion of Afghanistan was further welcomed by Saudi Arabia and the other Gulf states.

The Period 1979 to 1985

The final, and most cataclysmic phase of the Ba'th regime's Gulf policy is ongoing and will continue until the war with Iran comes to a conclusion—whether negotiated or otherwise. The origins of this half-decade-long conflict might well be traced to two developments that started this phase: the overthrow of the shah by Ayatollah Khomeini's Islamic revolution and the formal accession of Saddam Hussein to the leadership of Iraq. On July 16, 1979, President Ahmad Hasan al-Bakr resigned from the presidency on the grounds of ill health, and Saddam Hussein moved from the second to the first position in the state. His assumption of absolute power was accompanied by a purge of leading party figures—21 of those arrested were sentenced to death and 33 to prison terms. Some of those arrested were Hussein's protégés, and so far there has been no definitive explanation for these purges.[30] Nevertheless, some observers have linked both the timing of Saddam's inauguration and his purges to the crisis generated by the revolution in Iran.[31]

It is beyond debate that the most serious challenge to Iraq's stability and the Ba'thist regime's ambitions of playing a leading role in Arab and Gulf affairs has been the Islamic revolution in Iran and the subsequent war that erupted between the two countries. After the fall of the shah, Iraqi Foreign Minister Sa'dun Hammadi praised statements by Iranian Prime Minister Shahpur Bakhtiar that Iran would no longer play the role of Gulf policeman as "a positive step toward the establishment of cordial relations toward the Arab Gulf states."[32] Similar views were echoed by Saddam Hussein who told an Iraqi publication that Iraq was

> keen on cooperation with Iran in a way that will ensure the interests and security of the people in the area as well as preserve the historic ties based on noninterference and respect for national sovereignty. ... Any system which does not side with our enemy, respects our independence and whose oil policy is consistent with the interest of our two peoples will certainly command our respect and appreciation.[33]

Later, when Iranian leaders began harsh rhetorical attacks against Iraq, officials in Baghdad reasoned that the embryonic Iranian government should not be prematurely judged and even expressed hope for economic cooperation between the two countries.[34]

These hopes obviously did not materialize. Deep personal, ideological, territorial and strategic political differences continued to divide the two countries. There had been intense animosity between Saddam Hussein and Khomeini ever since Khomeini had been asked to leave Iraq for his antishah activities in the spring of 1978. More importantly, Khomeini believed that the Iranian revolution was the start of a regional, if not world, revolution to establish an international Islamic order. This ambition contradicted both Iraq's national sovereignty and the avowedly secular basis of the Ba'thist position. Saddam Hussein had stressed in 1977 that while his government revered the spiritual, historical, and cultural aspects of Iraq's Islamic heritage, it would not be enslaved by the past and was unalterably opposed to the "use of religion for political purposes lest it lead to sectarian and religious conflict."[35]

In the months that followed, the ideological exchange became increasingly heated. Iranian leaders called for a jihad to overthrow the "evil and atheist" Iraqi leadership, raising fears in the minds of Iraqi leaders that Iran might interfere in the ethnosectarian structure of Iraqi and Arab society. Iranian clerics also inveighed against Arab nationalism, one of the Ba'thist ideology's most basic tenets, charging that it contained not only Islamic but "Zionist, Facist and Nazi doctrines."[36] A turning point came when Iran began to support the al-Da'wa Party in committing acts of sabotage and assassination in Iraq.[37] Following an attempt on the life of Tariq Aziz, a member of the Revolutionary Command Council and the National and Regional

Commands of the party, by an Iraqi youth of Iranian origin, Iraq expelled thousands of Iranian residents and accused Khomeini of being a "turbaned shah" and using Islam to cover his "Persian racist designs" to destabilize and dominate the Gulf.[38]

Border skirmishes, infiltrations, and verbal attacks continued unabated until full-scale war erupted. By sending troops into Iran on September 22, 1980, Iraqi leaders appear to have sought several related goals:

1. to redress Iraq's perceived grievances over Shatt al-Arab and the land boundary areas that Iran refused to return to Iraq in accordance with the 1975 Algiers agreement;
2. to stop Iranian border incursions, attacks on border towns, infiltrations, and Iranian supported acts of sabotage;
3. to preempt the Iranian regime's threat to export its revolution to Iraq and to prevent it from interfering in internal Iraqi affairs and undermining the ethnosectarian structure of Iraqi society;
4. to overthrow Khomeini's government or to force it to come to the negotiating table at the time when it was widely perceived that Iran's army was divided, its arms obsolescent, and many of its officers under arrest;
5. to strengthen Iraq's aspirations for a regional role.

Predictions and fears about the war have vacillated wildly. At the outset, many experts predicted a rapid Iraqi victory and the dismemberment of Iran. All too quickly, however, many of the same analysts were predicting the collapse of the Iraqi regime. In a general sense, the conflict has now degenerated into a stalemate; a bitter and prolonged war of attrition in which neither side has the capability of winning a clear-cut victory. But if the hopes of Iraq's leaders for an immediate and decisive victory over Iran were quickly disillusioned, nevertheless, their aim of checking the spread of Khomeini's brand of Islamic fundamentalism to Iraq and other Arab states has been achieved at least for the time being.

And indeed, the issue of the war has been a central factor behind the major improvements that have occurred in the past few years in Iraq's relations with the Gulf countries, a development that could have serious long-term consequences for the future power configuration in the Gulf. The possible expansion of the conflict and Iran's intransigent position on continuing the war have come to be perceived as the greatest threat to local and regional security among the Arab Gulf countries. Although Iraq has not been received into the de facto alliance of the Arab Gulf countries, the Gulf Cooperation Council

(GCC), the GCC states perceive Iraq as their first line of defense and believe that if Iraq collapses they are likely to face a more menacing regime in Baghdad than Saddam's and a significantly less stable regional situation. Indeed, the evolution of Iraqi moderation and the persistence of Iran's tough rhetoric and action has produced a situation where the prospect of an Iraqi defeat would be met with strong Gulf Arab opposition. Saudi Crown Prince Abdullah put matters in a nutshell when he said two years ago: "Iran cannot enter Baghdad because that would mean an all-out Arab war with Iran."[39]

Initially, the Arab Gulf leaders viewed the war as an unfortunate dispute "between a brother and a friend,"[40] and in some cases, as a way to preoccupy the two regional giants. Still, they remained concerned about the impact of the war and its possible spread and therefore sought to remain as ostensibly neutral as possible so as not to antagonize Iran. But it eventually became quite clear that the Gulf states feared those of the consequences of an Iranian victory far more than they feared those of an Iraqi one. Iranian threats since the early days left their impact. Iranian attacks against the Gulf states reached high levels following the fall of the moderate government of Premier Mehdi Bazargan. The Iranian leaders accused Gulf states of being un-Islamic and as being nonindependent countries—mere satellites of the United States, and they pledged to support Islamic movements that would undermine these regimes.[41] Ayatollah Ruhani's threats to lead a movement to annex Bahrain unless the ruler accepted an "Islamic form of government" similar to Iran's and the suspected Iranian role in the December 1981 coup attempt were not forgotten. Nor were the Iranian air strikes against Kuwait in November 1980 and the more damaging air attack against Umm al-Aysh in 1981, which damaged millions of dollars worth of oil and storage facilities. There were also bombings in Kuwait in December 1983 against various embassies and installations, and more recently an attempt on the life of the emir of Kuwait. Responsibility for these activities were claimed by groups known to be supported by Iran, although the Iranians have denied any links to these incidents and have instead placed the blame on Iraq.

Although more recently Iran has had a hands-off attitude toward Bahrain and the other smaller states, Iranian enmity toward the Saudis increased to new levels in 1982. Iran has repeatedly tried to disrupt the pilgrimage to Makkah and Madinah and has also turned to economic warfare within OPEC against the Saudis. Recently ties improved slightly as Iranian officials visited Riyadh and the Saudi foreign minister visited Tehran in May 1985. Also recently, Iran has been following a policy of attempting to assure the Gulf states that they have nothing to fear from Iran if they halt their support for Iraq. Iranian envoys visited Bahrain, Qatar and the UAE, and the Iranian foreign minister revealed plans to visit Saudi Arabia. These events underscored the dilemma the Gulf states face of risking the danger of entanglement in the conflict against Iran, on the one hand, and doing what they can to prevent an Iranian victory, on the other.[42] But no basic change in attitude seems to have occurred and Iran continues to be the headquarters for a number of revolutionary organizations aiming to overthrow Gulf regimes. Thus Arab leaders appear to consider Khomeini as more of a threat than the shah.

The response of the Gulf states to these threats has varied. By the summer of 1981, Iraq had been promised extensive financial assistance from Kuwait and Saudi Arabia and had announced plans to build oil pipelines through these states.[43] Eventually, financial support from the Gulf states reached an estimated $25 billion in loans on very soft terms, among which was Kuwait's approval of a $2 billion dollar interest-free loan at the end of 1981. In 1982, in the wake of the pressures of declining oil revenues among the Gulf states, these sources of financial support apparently began to dry up. Shortly thereafter, oil industry sources reported that Iraq began receiving financial assistance from Saudi Arabia, Kuwait, and other Gulf states in the form of sales proceeds from roughly 300 thousand b/d of crude oil, mostly sold to Japanese customers. It was reported in late 1985, however, that the Saudis and the Kuwaitis were planning to end their agreement to sell the 300 thousand b/d on behalf of Iraq once the year's contracts were fulfilled. The two countries were reported to have informed Iran of the decision through OPEC channels. Iran had previously protested this support of Iraq on the part of Saudi Arabia and Kuwait. If implemented, this decision would appear to have been linked to the completion of the strategic pipeline carrying Iraqi oil to Yanbu, which is scheduled to carry 500 thousand b/d by the end of 1985.[44] Although this economic aid is of critical importance to Iraq, it is much less than the reported $1 billion per month provided by Gulf neighbors during much of 1981 and 1982.[45]

Hence, after a half-decade of hostility, the Gulf states' attitude, is crystallizing—the war must end and the fundamental question remains how to influence Iran. The Gulf states lack sufficient influence with both sides, but they can influence events to a certain extent by active diplomacy, by giving political and economic support to Iraq, and possibly by giving large amounts of aid to help in the reconstruction of the two countries as one way of influencing Iran.

Moreover, Iraq's relations with the Gulf states are better than they have been at any time in recent history, and not simply as a result of regional concerns about the Gulf war and the Iranian revolution. Rather, Iraq's foreign policy in general and its Gulf policy in particular have become more tactful and less rigid than before. In the Gulf, Iraq's pragmatism and use of skillful diplomacy have combined with political expediency to produce a convergence of its interests with those of the other Arab Gulf states in the context of the war. The evolution in the thinking of Iraqi leaders, which started in the mid-seventies, is in essence the conceptualization of foreign policy as an instrument to achieve regional accommodation rather than to pursue regional ideological transformation.

This visionary approach to foreign policy is reflected in Iraq's ties of economic cooperation with the Gulf states. For example, Saudi Arabia has allowed Iraq to build a strategic oil pipeline to the Red Sea, and Kuwait has made a similar agreement. A network of railroads and superhighways is also planned to link Iraq to Kuwait, Syria, Lebanon, Jordan, and other Gulf countries. In addition, Baghdad has pursued several forms of agricultural cooperation with Gulf states, a sector of great potential productivity. Two of the steps Baghdad has taken are (1) the liberalization of Iraqi laws to enable private Gulf investment in agricultural projects in Iraq (particularly in poultry and livestock farming) and (2) Iraq's active participation in the Conference of Ministers of Agriculture of the Gulf States and Arabian Peninsula, which has approved an estimated $100 million of grain and grain seed production projects. In addition, joint Iraqi-Gulf industrial projects have been set up, which extend beyond government-to-government schemes to include private Gulf investment in small- to medium-sized manufacturing projects in Iraq. Also, contractors from Iraq and other Gulf states are working increasingly in each other's territories, and steps have been taken to increase cooperation in the areas of trade, transport, and tourism.[46]

Moreover, in moves that link foreign policy to political stability and economic development, Iraq has in recent years become involved in a number of Gulf economic institutions. It has said that it will participate in all ventures sponsored by the Doha-based Gulf Organization for Industrial Consulting, which was set up in 1976 by Iraq, Bahrain, Oman, Kuwait, Qatar, Saudi Arabia, and the UAE to carry out feasibility studies, in addition to being party to the Riyadh-based Conference of Gulf and Arabian Peninsula Agriculture Ministers, the Kuwait-based Arab-Maritime Petroleum Transport Companies, the United Arab Shipping Company, and other institutions. Furthermore, Iraq is included in some of the practical plans of the Gulf Cooperation Council. For example, UAE Oil Minister Mana Saeed al-Otaiba has said that one of the aims of the GCC is to build a major pipeline network extending "all the way from southern Iraq, through Kuwait, Saudi Arabia, Qatar and Dubai, and heading out into the Gulf of Oman. When not carrying oil this network could be used to pipe fresh water from the Shatt al-Arab to the desert further south."[47]

Iraq was not invited, however, to join the GCC because of the "special relations and similarities" existing among the states of the Arabian peninsula, and because the Gulf states did not want to appear as if they were ganging up on Iran. On the other hand, the Iraqis have said that they favor any cooperative or unionist Arab efforts as long as they do not lead to the establishment of opposing Arab axes or blocs, oppose the principles of the Arab League, or permit foreign influences or presence into the Arab world.[48] Hence, too much should not be made of Iraq's current exclusion from the GCC. Her links with the Gulf, while part of Iraq's goal of Arab economic integration, are unlike Iraq's ties with other Arab states. They appear to be better studied, more diverse, and more substantial and to derive in no small part from Iraq's more pragmatic and flexible approach to the Gulf countries—an approach, now roughly a decade old, based on economic and security interests. As the war continues—and with it Iraq's pragmatism and Khomeini's extremism—Iraq's approach can only magnify further the impact its current positive relations with the Gulf countries will have on its long-term role in the area.

The Future of Iraqi-Gulf Relations

Although all predictions about the duration and course of the Iran-Iraq war must be made with extreme caution, it is crucial that Iraq achieve a face-saving settlement. In the fall of 1985, the best Baghdad can hope for is a political settlement with Iran that will not sacrifice or unduly impair the political power of Saddam Hussein's regime. It is more likely, however, that there will be no negotiated settlement as long as Khomeini and Saddam remain in power.

Whatever the future course of the war, events to date leave no doubt that, once it ends, Iraq will have to work out a new kind of relationship with Iran and the Gulf states. But what kind of arrangements are likely to emerge? Is the GCC likely to survive in its current form or will Iraq, and possibly the Yemens, be included as members or somehow become associated in a less formal manner? Is it too farfetched to see some future arrangement in which even Iran would be given a role? When and if a peaceful settlement is reached, are the countries of the region likely to avoid confrontation and concentrate on the economic, social, and political challenges posed by transition to modern societies?

If the war ends with neither side achieving a decisive victory, Iraq and Iran would be left to renew their competition for regional influence over other, smaller states of the region. For the Iraqi regime, however, the primary concern over the next few years will continue to be Iran. Unless the two sides recognize that their interests require noninterference in each other's internal affairs and equal access to Shatt al-Arab, this conflict with roots in history, sovereignty, security, ideology, and nationalism is likely to remain a tacit or actual casus belli.

Consequently, Iraq will have a strong interest in maintaining good and close relations with the Arab states of the Gulf, and it is unlikely that Baghdad would jeopardize the better ties it has found with its Arab neighbors by reverting to earlier, aggressive policies. The ties with countries such as Egypt, Jordan, and Saudi Arabia are likely to endure. Iraq's gratitude for the support provided by these countries and Gulf states, such as Kuwait, and its continued dependence on them for commercial and transit arrangements are likely to eliminate any chances of reverting to the era of confrontation.

The improvement in its ties with its neighbors and with the United States, in the context of maturing recognition of its real capabilities, is likely to encourage Iraq to maintain policies of moderation. Iraqi Foreign Minister Tariq Aziz reflected this attitude when he recently told a group of U.S. congressman that the policy of seeking regional domination by one leader or country in the area is outdated, and cooperation is the path of the future.[49] In fact, the war has been a major catalyst in Iraqi thinking, and the Iraqis are fearful that moving against the Gulf states would make them vulnerable to an Iranian threat. In addition, with a hostile Iran to the east and a rival Syrian Ba'th to the west, Iraqis are not likely to take actions that will lead the Gulf countries to make common cause with Iran or with Syria and to set up a new hostile frontier.

In domestic terms, if the Iraqi regime survives the war basically intact, it is likely to continue to emphasize economic development at home and to push for a broader domestic political consensus to support the credible regional role its leaders aspire to. There is unlikely to be any substantial change in Iraq's long-term plans for internal social and economic development, which means Iraq's leaders must concentrate on reconstruction and development of the country's oil resources. In other words, the domestic outlook for the Ba'th regime, given its medium- and long-term political and economic aims, will militate strongly against future adventurism in the Gulf, or elsewhere. Indeed, Iraq's future regional and global importance derives from its unique capacity, relative to other Middle East countries, for long-term economic and social development based on both oil and non-oil resources, particularly agriculture. Hence, Iraqi leaders are likely to work hard to avoid the regional isolation and hostility they faced during the first years of the Ba'th's return to power.

In addition, security and regional stability are important goals for the present Iraqi leadership. Arguably, Iraq's attack on Iran stemmed as much from these objectives as from any others. Since the middle and late 1970s, the Iraqis have cooperated with Jordan, Saudi Arabia, and some of the Gulf states on a variety of issues. Hostility against the Gulf states does not fit with the Iraqi regime's interest in stability. Iraq's political ties with the Gulf are likely to remain constructive for years as long as there are no radical changes in either Baghdad or Riyadh or in the smaller states of the Gulf. The Iraqis are not likely to play a large role in the Gulf unless they are invited to do so by the Gulf states themselves, which probably will not happen unless there is a perception of Iranian or other threats to the region that requires Iraq's support. In an interview with Kuwaiti journalists, Saddam Hussein was asked about the possible establishment of a local, Gulf-based rapid deployment force. He responded, "We don't want to consider ourselves a Gulf state except when you tell us, 'You are a sister Gulf state.' Iraq is Arab. Iraq lies on the Gulf. But Iraq is not looking for external appearances and only wants good for its sister countries and anytime you think we are good enough to be included as a sister Gulf state on any level of cooperation, we will study the offer and act in accordance with our national principles."[50]

One possible option, though somewhat improbable, is the inclusion of Iraq in the GCC or in an Arab Gulf security pact to face future threats that might result from a regional conflagration, such as a new Arab-Israeli war, eruption of a new inter-Gulf conflict, or subversion attempts supported by external powers. Juxtaposed with this possibility are potential problem areas that could lead to a deterioration in Iraqi-Gulf relations. Iraq and the GCC states, while favoring the maintenance of Gulf security by local power, may have different outlooks on how to achieve such a goal. Iraq's relations with Kuwait and the conflict over the islands of Warba and Bubyan could complicate ties. Conflict may erupt over how to deal with Iran, particularly if a less hostile regime is ruling in Tehran.

Nevertheless, the fundamental conclusion to be drawn is that the Iraqi regime seems to have tempered its long-term ideological goals with short-term programs. It has exhibited a combination of constant strategic goals and flexible tactics that has served it well. Unless it is excluded from economic and political participation in the region, Iraq will continue to pursue economic development at home, regional economic integration with other Gulf states, a nonaligned foreign policy, and a broad domestic consensus that would allow it to play an appropriately active regional role. If Iraq's interests are ignored and if it is isolated, its role is likely to become negative and disruptive. Iraq would then be inclined to interfere in GCC affairs or to deepen conflicts among its members. Again, a full or associate membership within the GCC would make Iraq more responsible, that is, easier to contain from within than without.

Another even less probable scenario could emerge. Iraq and Iran, following Khomeini's death or the end of the war, could come to the realization that neither can emerge as the dominant power in the region. Their respective national interests and the lessons of the war might convince them of the need to suppress their long-term tensions and terminate the constant squandering of their human and material resources. In these circumstances, the two sides would sign a peace treaty and work closely with other Gulf states to transform the Gulf into a zone of peace and to exclude superpower presence in the Gulf by setting up an organization to guarantee regional security by the local powers.

Notes

1. *The Economist*, June 6, 1981.
2. *Al Jumhurriya* (Baghdad), July 21, 1980.
3. Christine Moss Helms, *Iraq: Eastern Flank of the Arab World* (Washington, D.C.: The Brookings Institution, 1984), 108.
4. *Al-Istiqlal* (Baghdad), "Iraq's duty toward the Arab Emirates," February 7, 1939.
5. *Al-Istiqlal* (Baghdad), September 21 and 23, 1934.
6. Majid Khadduri, *Independent Iraq* (London: Oxford University Press, 1951), 141. See also Mustafa al-Najjar, *Al-Tarikh al-Siyassi li-Alaqat al-Iraq al-Dawliyya bil-Khalij* (Basra: Basra University Press, 1975).
7. Abd al-Razzaq al-Harani, *Tarikh al-Wazarat al-Iraqiyya* (Beirut: Dar al-Kuttub Press, 1974), vol. 3, pp. 323–330.
8. Majid Khadduri, *Independent Iraq*, 2nd ed. (London: Oxford University Press, 1966), 161. Khadduri's trilogy—*Independent Iraq, Republican Iraq, A Study in Iraqi Politics since the Revolution of 1958* (London: Oxford University Press, 1969) and *Socialist Iraq, A Study in Iraqi Politics since 1968* (Washington, D.C.: Middle East Institute, 1978)—remains to this day the most authoritative work on modern Iraqi history and politics.
9. For details of the Kurdish debate, see Khadduri, *Republican Iraq*, 2nd ed., 1–10.
10. Ibid., 160–168.
11. Tim Niblock, "Iraq Policies towards the Arab States of the Gulf: 1958–1981," in *Iraq: The Contemporary State*, edited by Tim Niblock (New York: St. Martin's Press, 1982), 132–139.

12. For discussion of the Ba'th Party, see Kamil Abu Jabir, *Arab Ba'th Socialist Party* (Syracuse, N.Y.: Syracuse University Press, 1966); John Devlin, *The Ba'th Party* (Stanford, Calif.: Hoover Institution Press, 1976); and Khadduri, *Republican Iraq, Socialist Iraq,* and *Political Trends in the Arab World* (Baltimore: Johns Hopkins University, 1972) and *Arab Contemporaries* (Baltimore: Johns Hopkins University Press, 1973).

13. *Revolutionary Iraq,* the political report adopted by the 8th Regional Conference of the Ba'th Party, Baghdad, October 1974, 206.

14. Khadduri, *Revolutionary Iraq,* 207–208.

15. Ibid., 89.

16. Edmund Ghareeb, "Iraq: Emergent Gulf Power," in *The Security of the Persian Gulf,* edited by Hossein Amirsadeghi (London: Croom Helm, 1981), 205; and "Iraq and Gulf Security," in *The Impact of Iranian Events Upon U.S. and Persian Gulf Serenity* (Washington, D.C.: American Foreign Policy Institute, 1979).

17. *Al-Jumhurriyya* (Baghdad), October 13, 1969.

18. S. Chubin and S. Zabih, *The Foreign Relations of Iran* (Berkeley and Los Angeles, Calif.: University of California Press, 1974), 195.

19. For details on the Kurdish question during this phase, see Edmund Ghareeb, *The Kurdish Question in Iraq* (Syracuse, N.Y.: Syracuse University Press, 1981).

20. *Middle East Economic Digest,* November 29, 1974.

21. *Al-Hawadith* (Beirut), December 27, 1974.

22. *Al-Nahar* (Beirut), March 19, 1975.

23. Ghassan Salameh, *Al-Siyasah al-Kharijiyya al-Saudiyya Munthu 1945 [Saudi Foreign Policy since 1945]* Beirut: Ma'had al-Inma al-Arabi, 1980), 75.

24. *Al-Nahar* (Beirut), February 26, 1976.

25. *Arab Report and Record,* December 16–31, 1976.

26. Joint Saudi-Kuwaiti Communique, in *News from Saudi Arabia,* March 30, 1976.

27. *Newsweek* interview with Crown Prince Fahd, March 26, 1979.

28. J. M. Abdulghani, *Iraq and Iran: Years of Crisis* (London: Croom Helm, 1984), 194–195.

29. Ibid., 195.

30. *Al-Thawra* (Baghdad), February 12, 1980.

31. See Edward Mortimer, *Faith and Power: The Politics of Islam* (New York: Vintage Books, 1982), 364–365.

32. *Al-Hawadith* (London), April 18, 1980.

33. *Baghdad Observer,* February 27, 1979.

34. Author's interview with Revolutionary Command Council member and Deputy Prime Minister Naim Haddad, Baghdad, April 1979.

35. Cited in Amir Iskander, *Saddam Hussein* (Paris: Hachette, 1980), 159.

36. *Le Monde,* April 8, 1980.

37. Al-Da'wa was founded in the 1960s by some Shi'ite religious leaders who resented the secular feature of the Ba'th regime.

38. Edmund Ghareeb, "The Forgotten War," *American-Arab Affairs,* 5 (Summer 1983): 63–64. See also Abdulghani, *Iraq and Iran,* 188–193.

39. Interview conducted by *Al-Siyasa* (Kuwait) and translated in Foreign Broadcast Information Service, *Daily Report: Middle East and Africa,* March 23, 1983, p. C5.

40. Helms, *Iraq: Eastern Flank,* p. 180.

41. For details, see Abdulghani, *Iraq and Iran,* 197.

42. *Al-Ittihad* (Abu Dhabi), October 15, 1985.

43. Naomi Sakr, "Economic Relations between Iraq and Other Arab Gulf States," in *Iraq: The Contemporary State,* edited by Tim Niblock, 150.

44. *Al-Sharq al-Awsat* (London), October 7, 1985.

45. *Outlook for International Oil Markets,* Wharton Middle East Economic Service, January 1984, p. 12.

46. Sakr, "Economic Relations," 162–164.

47. Iraqi News Agency, March 2, 1980.

48. Author's interview with a high-ranking Ba'thist official, October 1981.

49. According to congressional sources, this statement was made in meetings held in Washington in November of 1984.

50. *Al-Thawrah* (Baghdad), May 5, 1984.

5

Iraq and the Superpowers

Mark N. Katz

Ever since the July 1958 revolution, Iraq has had close ties, for the most part, to the Soviet Union. A treaty of friendship and cooperation exists between Moscow and Baghdad, and the Soviets have sent both arms and advisers to Iraq for many years. At the outset of the Iran-Iraq war, however, the Soviets stopped sending weapons to Iraq directly and took other actions favoring Iran. The Kremlin returned to sending arms to Iraq once Iranian troops crossed into Iraq in 1982 and it was clear that Tehran was not responding favorably to Moscow's overtures. Since mid-1984, however, Iran has begun to be more responsive to Moscow, and Soviet-Iranian relations have improved somewhat.

Although dependent on the USSR for military supplies, Iraq has had reason to be unhappy with Soviet behavior. Since the mid-1970s, and especially since the outbreak of the war, Iraq has expanded its relations with the West even to the point where Baghdad has purchased sophisticated weapons from France. In late 1984, Baghdad and Washington restored diplomatic relations that Iraq had broken off in 1967. Is Iraq moving away from the USSR and toward the United States and the West, or is it retaining close ties to the East while improving them with the West? How firm is Baghdad's longstanding friendship with Moscow and its budding one with Washington? How will Iraq's relations with both superpowers evolve over the next three years? Obviously, a definitive answer cannot be given to what will happen in the future, but through looking at Iraq's relations with the United States and the USSR in the past, we may gain a better understanding of the conditions under which Baghdad may draw toward or away from each superpower.

The Past and the Present[1]

Before the collapse of the Ottomans in 1918, Iraq was ruled as part of that empire. After World War I, Britain governed Iraq under a League of Nations mandate. The British installed a member of the Hashemite family as king (as they did also in Transjordan and, unsuccessfully, in Syria). Iraq gained its independence in 1932, and the royal government was strongly pro-Western. In 1944, Iraq established diplomatic relations with Moscow, but 10 years later Baghdad broke them. In 1955, Iraq along with Turkey, Iran, Pakistan, and Britain signed the Baghdad Pact, the major purpose of which was to prevent the spread of Marxism in Southwest Asia. The Iraqi monarchy was heavily criticized for its military alliance with the West not only by radical Arab leaders such as Nasser but also moderate ones like King Sa'ud. The Hashemite monarchy was overthrown in July 1958 in a coup led by General Qasim who immediately changed Iraq's foreign policy from a pro-Western to a pro-Soviet orientation. In 1958–1959, Qasim withdrew Iraq from the Baghdad Pact, cancelled an Anglo-Iraqi security agreement, and ousted the last remaining British soldiers. Relations with Moscow were quickly restored and soon Soviet arms and instructors began to arrive. While not broken, Baghdad's ties to Washington deteriorated sharply, especially as U.S. support for the shah of Iran increased in the late 1950s and early 1960s. The Soviets were neutral at first when Qasim claimed Kuwait as part of Iraqi territory because Moscow's other Arab ally, Nasser, opposed this move. When the Kuwaitis called for British assistance, though, the Soviets denounced this move and gave political support to Iraq.

When the Ba'th Party seized power for the first time in February 1963, Soviet-Iraqi relations declined sharply as the Ba'th and the Iraqi Communist Party fought against each other. Soviet military aid to Baghdad ceased and was only restored to its former level after the November 1963 coup which ousted the Ba'thists and brought General Arif to power.

Although close to the Soviets, General Arif's relations with the United States were less hostile than Qasim's. The Iraqis were not pleased when their Soviet ally moved closer to the shah of Iran for a brief period in the 1960s. Baghdad's rapprochement with Washington, however, was limited, due to U.S. support of Israel, and ended completely as a result of the 1967 Arab-Israeli war. When the Ba'th came to power again in 1968 (under the leadership of General al-Bakr), the Soviets did not have the same problems with them that they had in 1963. In a step that Moscow heartily approved, the Ba'th in 1973 formed a National Front uniting other parties, including the powerful Iraqi Communist Party. Iraq's animosity toward the United States was a result not only of U.S. aid to Israel in both the 1967 and the 1973 Middle East wars, but also of increased U.S support to the shah of Iran who had in turn begun supporting Kurdish forces to resist Baghdad's authority.

Iraq turned toward the Soviets more closely than ever in order to obtain arms and advisers to support its efforts to counter the Kurds. In 1972, Baghdad and Moscow signed a 20 year treaty of friendship and cooperation. This, along with Iraqi support to Marxist rebels in Oman, encouraged the United States to see Iraq as a Soviet ally and to send more arms and advisers to pro-Western governments in Iran and Saudi Arabia. But instead of leading to an even closer Soviet-Iraqi alliance, the next few years saw Baghdad reduce its dependence on Moscow. The dramatic oil price rise of 1973 gave Iraq the ability to import more from the West and not rely so much on Eastern bloc trade and aid. The 1975 Iran-Iraq agreement that resolved (for a time) the border issue and ended Tehran's support to the Kurds meant that Baghdad could reduce its reliance on Soviet military assistance.

Iraq did indeed appear to become more independent of the Soviets in the mid-1970s, but this did not improve U.S.-Iraqi ties. Baghdad frequently condemned the United States for its support of Israel and called for a comprehensive Middle East peace settlement at the same time that Washington saw Iraq as one of the leading supporters of PLO terrorist groups. In the late 1970s, Iraqi-Soviet relations deteriorated somewhat as Baghdad openly criticized several Soviet foreign policy actions. In the Horn of Africa conflict of 1977–1978, Iraq sided with Somalia while the Soviets and Cubans aided Ethiopia. Later, Iraq (along with most other Arab governments) backed the Eritrean guerrillas against Soviet-supported Ethiopian forces. Iraq also disapproved of the pro-Soviet coup that took place in South Yemen in June 1978, and Iraqi-South Yemeni relations quickly deteriorated. The April 1978 Marxist coup in Afghanistan particularly worried the Ba'th government and may well have contributed to its decision to oust the Iraqi Communist Party from the National Front and to execute or imprison many of its members. The Soviets were not happy with this move, but could do little to help the Iraqi communists if Moscow's ties to Baghdad were to be preserved.

Yet despite this growing hostility toward the Soviet Union, U.S.-Iraqi relations did not improve. If anything, they grew worse after the signing of the U.S.-sponsored Camp David accords in 1978. Moscow was able to use this event to improve relations with Baghdad on the basis of a common anti-American policy. With the fall of the shah and the rise of Ayatollah Khomeini at the beginning of 1979, Iraq was faced with a different foreign policy challenge than before. Iran was no longer allied to the United States, but its Shi'a Islamic revolutionary government posed a potential threat to Iraq, where

more than half the population is also Shi'a but the government has
been dominated by Sunnis. The Ba'th government had sheltered
Ayatollah Khomeini for many years, but expelled him shortly before
the shah fell. When Khomeini arrived in Iran from France, he declared
Saddam Hussein and the Ba'th government to be one of his opponents.
The Iraqis were not pleased when Moscow rushed to make friends
with the new Tehran government.[2] Iraq's attitude toward the USSR
grew even cooler after the Soviet invasion of Afghanistan at the end
of 1979 and Baghdad joined most other Islamic nations in condemning
Moscow for this action. When Iraq invaded Iran in September 1980,
the USSR did not assist its allies in Baghdad but instead halted direct
arms transfers to Iraq and in the following month signed a treaty of
friendship and cooperation with Iraq's rival, Syria (which openly
backed Iran).[3] It was widely reported that the USSR even sent some
arms to Iran directly across their common border or sent weapons
through North Korea. Yet even in this extreme situation, Iraq did not
break relations or abrogate its treaty with Moscow. Nor did Iraq move
closer to the United States. Both superpowers proclaimed their neutrality in the Iran-Iraq war. But whereas the United States had relations
with neither party (U.S. ties with Iran were broken in 1979 at the
time of the seizure of the American embassy in Tehran), the Soviets
had ties with both. At the beginning of the war, Moscow sided with
Tehran; they did not approve of their ally Iraq attacking a state with
an anti-American government that they hoped to become friends
with. Moscow, however, did not completely abandon its old friend
in its attempt to win a new one; there were reports that Soviet arms
were reaching Iraq through third parties. Soviet ships brought arms
to the Jordanian port of Aqaba to be transferred over land to Iraq.
According to William Quandt, the Saudis allowed Soviet arms to be
landed at a Saudi port and transshipped across their territory to Iraq
even though the Saudis do not even have diplomatic relations with
Moscow and are extremely anti-Soviet.[4]

Tehran, however, did not respond to Moscow's offers of friendship.
The ayatollah denounced Moscow as "the other Satan," gave some
assistance to the Afghan mujahiddin, and crushed the growing power
of the Tudeh (the Iranian communist party). As the tide of war turned
and the Iranians forced the Iraqis to retreat and then crossed into
Iraqi territory themselves, the Soviets began to reassess their position
on the war. They undoubtedly realized that if the Iranians defeated
Iraq or forced the Ba'th out of office, Moscow would see a friendly
regime replaced by a less friendly (perhaps hostile) Islamic fundamentalist one. The Soviets also saw that the spread of Islamic fundamentalism threatened not only pro-American governments in the

region, but also pro-Soviet ones. Finally, the Soviets must have been concerned about the possibility of Islamic fundamentalism spreading to their own Moslem population in Central Asia. At some point in 1982, then, Moscow agreed to resume arms transfers to Baghdad.[5]

So long as Iraqi forces were in Iran, the United States attempted to follow a neutral policy toward the combatants. Once Iranian forces entered Iraq, however, a debate arose in Washington over what the United States should do. Some wanted to continue the policy of strict neutrality for fear of otherwise getting dragged into a long, drawn-out conflict. Others argued that the United States should tilt toward Iraq because, if Iraq were defeated, the oil-rich Gulf Cooperation Council states (which did not have the same defensive capability as Iraq) would be vulnerable to Iranian attack. At first the Reagan administration appeared to opt for the former policy and tried hard to prevent the French from selling Exocet missiles to Iraq because Iran had threatened to block the Strait of Hormuz if Iraq used these missiles. By the beginning of 1984, however, the latter policy appeared to prevail when the United States sent a naval task force to the Gulf in order to deter Iran from its threat against the Strait. With increasing recognition in Washington of the importance to U.S. interests in not seeing Iraq defeated, and with Baghdad's desire to encourage the United States to undertake policies such as discouraging U.S. allies from selling arms to Iran (as well as desiring widening contacts with the United States and the West), U.S-Iraqi diplomatic relations were restored at the end of 1984.[6]

The Soviets have responded to this steady improvement in U.S.-Iraqi relations by attempting to improve their ties to Iran. Since mid-1984, Moscow has apparently met with some success. High-level Soviet-Iranian meetings have taken place and trade has grown. More important, it appears that the Soviets have begun providing some security assistance to Tehran, though what kind and how much are uncertain. Although unhappy about this, Iraq remains outwardly friendly toward the USSR as it did during the early part of the war when the USSR leaned toward Iran.[7]

The Future

From looking at Iraq's past relations with the superpowers, it is clear that although Baghdad has had close links with Moscow since the late 1950s, the Soviets have often undertaken foreign policy actions that displeased or actually harmed Iraq. Given this history, it is doubtful that the Iraqis are as enthusiastic allies of the USSR as the South Yemenis are. At the same time, the Iraqi armed forces have relied on Soviet military equipment. It would be extremely difficult for Baghdad to break with Moscow the way Egypt and Somalia have, not only because of the enormous costs of resupplying its armed forces with Western military equipment, but also because Iraq could not be certain of obtaining equivalent supplies of weapons from the West as long as the Iran-Iraq war continues.[8]

How are Iraqi relations with the superpowers likely to evolve over the next few years? Under what conditions would Iraq draw closer to either one or be distant from both? This very much depends on the course of events and the policies of the two superpowers. What these conditions are will be examined under two cases: if the war continues and if the war ends.

The more likely case is that the war will continue. So long as it does, Iraq will undoubtedly attempt to maintain as good a relationship as possible with the Soviet Union, for Iraq is heavily dependent on Soviet weapons to continue the war effort, especially since Baghdad has been on the defensive. Iraq simply cannot afford to give up the weapons supply, and therefore Baghdad's growing friendship with the United States cannot be expected to lead Iraq to break with Moscow—unless the Soviets undertook actions extremely hostile to Iraq, like unilaterally breaking ties with Baghdad. This, however, does not seem likely. A more likely situation to end the Soviet-Iraqi friendship would be a Soviet cessation of arms shipments to Iraq as well as the commencement of large-scale, direct arms transfers and military assistance to Iran. Under these circumstances, the Iraqis would have little choice but to try to obtain arms as quickly as possible from the West.

Part of the reason Moscow stopped leaning toward Iran in 1982–1983 was that Tehran simply did not respond favorably toward the Soviets. Recently, however, Iran has been more receptive to the Kremlin's friendly overtures. There is some concern that this trend may continue and that the Soviets may indeed heavily arm Tehran. The Soviets have long argued that Moscow and Tehran should work together "against imperialism" (the United States). With the Soviets behind them, revolutionary Iran could pose a much more serious threat to the pro-Western GCC states than it now does. With Soviet assistance, for example, it would be much more difficult for the United States to prevent Iran from carrying out its longstanding threat to close the Strait of Hormuz.

The conclusion of a Soviet-Iranian alliance is unlikely though, and for several reasons. First, there appears to be a natural limit on the degree to which Iran and the USSR can cooperate. The ayatollah's government crushed the Tudeh and is unlikely to allow Soviet influence to grow to the point where it could significantly affect Iranian internal politics. In addition, the USSR and Iran are basically competitors for influence in the neighboring countries. Iran would like to see Islamic fundamentalism come to power in Iraq and the Arabian peninsula. Moscow would be happy to see pro-Western governments in the region fall, but would not like to see fundamentalist governments hostile to Moscow replace them. For Islamic fundamentalism threatens not only pro-Western governments, but also pro-Soviet ones such as those in Afghanistan, South Yemen, and Syria. And if Islamic fundamentalism were to begin to spread, Moscow would find it difficult to keep Soviet Central Asia immune.

Less dramatically, the Soviets do not have an interest in seeing Islamic fundamentalism replace the Ba'th government in Iraq. The Kremlin has no guarantee that a Baghdad government allied to Tehran would be as closely tied to Moscow as the Ba'th government now is. Further, it has been Moscow's position all along that it would like to see a peaceful solution to the Iran-Iraq war. Ideally, though perhaps unrealistically, the USSR would like to be friends with both Iraq and Iran. The Soviets have attempted to maintain friendship with both parties to local disputes before, as with North and South Yemen (1972 and 1979), Ethiopia and Somalia (1977), and India and Pakistan (1965). As seen in the latter two cases, such a policy does not always succeed, although this does not prevent the Soviets from continuing to try. The Soviets would very much like to be the party that successfully mediates between Iran and Iraq, but if Khomeini keeps on insisting that Saddam Hussein must leave office, Soviet peace efforts will probably fail. Moscow may also find it useful to make friends in Tehran now in order to be in a better position to exert its influence when Ayatollah Khomeini finally dies. The Kremlin might see this as a significant advantage as Washington is not in a position to do the same due to the complete rupture in U.S.-Iranian relations in 1979 and Tehran's extreme anti-Americanism. If the Soviets can get Iran to reduce its aid to the Afghan guerrillas, to increase its trade with the USSR, and generally to be friendlier toward the USSR, Moscow may feel that its minimum goals in Iran have been met. Moreover Iraq is not likely to cease relying on the USSR if Moscow improves its relations with Tehran without giving it large-scale military assistance.

Yet just because Iraq must depend on the USSR does not mean that Baghdad is happy over Moscow's flirtation with Tehran or support to Damascus. Friendship with the United States is desirable to Baghdad so that Washington will not hinder Iraq's effort to obtain arms from other Western states. The United States will also remain very important to Iraq as it works more vigorously to stop its other allies from selling arms to Iran.

Should the war continue, then, and the Soviets do not give large-scale military aid to Tehran, Iraq is likely both to maintain its close ties to the USSR in order to continue receiving Soviet weapons and to build ties to the United States. It is useful to Iraq to be friends with both.

It is much more difficult to discuss how Iraq's relations with the superpowers might evolve if the war ended soon because it seems so unlikely and it is so uncertain how it will end. There are several possibilities, and each could significantly affect what happens. The Iran-Iraq war in many ways resembles World War I with its great losses but relatively static positions. Perhaps as in that war, the loser will not be militarily defeated, but rather will be the first to collapse internally. If Iraq collapses first and Tehran can take advantage of the situation to promote a Shi'a Islamic fundamentalist group to power in Baghdad, Iraq's future relations with the two superpowers would depend on Iran's relations with them. And Tehran may well prefer that Baghdad not have strong ties with either the United States or the Soviet Union. If Iran is the first to collapse, a struggle for power could emerge in Tehran in which the Soviet Union, the United States, and perhaps Iraq (as well as others) would attempt to influence the outcome. Even if one united group overthrew the Khomeini regime, both Washington and Moscow would move quickly to befriend it, if this were possible. With its larger population as well as its geographic position that both borders the USSR and occupies the entire northern coast of the Gulf including the vital Strait of Hormuz, Iran really is strategically more important to both superpowers than Iraq. Although Moscow and Washington both would like to be friends with Iraq, each would undoubtedly consider friendship or alliance with Iran as more important and would be willing to risk poorer relations with Baghdad to be the dominant influence in Tehran. If there were a change of regime in Iran, Iraqi-Iranian hostility could also decline; but nonetheless, if one superpower had stronger ties with Iran, Iraq would still find it prudent to seek the support of the other.

It is also possible that the war could end through military victory for one side or the other. If Iran were to defeat Iraq, the same considerations as when Iraq collapsed internally would apply, even more strongly. Iran would be the dominant power and neither superpower would have much influence in Baghdad. Because the next most likely target of an Iranian desire to spread Islamic revolution would be the pro-Western GCC states, Iran would be more likely to come into conflict with the United States than the USSR. But the unpredictable leaders in Tehran could decide to turn their attention to Afghanistan instead. At present, it appears next to impossible that Iraq could defeat Iran after having failed to do this at the beginning of the war and having had to defend its own territory for some time now.

Other changes that could occur include the Ba'th Party ousting Saddam Hussein or the Iraqi military overthrowing the Ba'th Party in an effort to satisfy Khomeini and induce him to end the war. The crucial question, of course, is whether the ayatollah would accept this or would insist that an Islamic fundamentalist government come to power in addition to these changes. Neither the Ba'th nor the Iraqi military could be expected to acquiesce to this. A new Ba'th or military government would probably continue on the same foreign policy course toward both the superpowers; it would have little incentive to give up its ties to either.

The war could also come to an end if the Ayatollah Khomeini died in the near future and the new Iranian leadership dropped the demand that Saddam Hussein leave office. This would be the best opportunity for a peaceful settlement of the conflict. If this indeed occurred, Iraq would probably want to have good relations with both the USSR and the United States, but would perhaps place greater emphasis initially on ties to Washington as Baghdad would have less need for arms while a great need for investment and economic assistance from the West and the pro-Western Arab states in restoring its economy.[9] Poor relations with the United States would be counterproductive for Iraq's reconstruction effort, which would probably take several years. But as in the case where a new government arose in Tehran after political collapse in Iran, Baghdad would be extremely concerned over the probable competition between the superpowers to make friends with Khomeini's successors.

Yet even if a peaceful settlement to the war were to lead Iraq to seek better relations with the United States during the reconstruction period, Iraq would probably at some point reassert its claim to the leadership of the Arab world. In the highly likely event that the Arab-Israeli conflict persists and the United States continues to support Israel, Iraq can be expected to distance itself from the United States and perhaps become more pro-Soviet. The future of U.S-Iraqi relations will also be affected by the extent to which Iraq cooperates with or opposes U.S plans to defend the Persian Gulf region. In the past, the two have not cooperated on this issue because Washington regarded Baghdad as a close ally of Moscow, and hence one of the threats to stability in the Gulf.

Still another possibility is that the Soviet rapprochement with Iran succeeds and Khomeini himself is persuaded to drop his demand for Saddam Hussein's ouster and to negotiate a peaceful settlement. If the USSR were able to bring about a negotiated settlement between Baghdad and Khomeini or his successors, the Soviets would probably appear to be the most politically powerful superpower in Iran and Iraq. If the Iranian government remained anti-American but became friendlier toward the USSR, Baghdad may well turn to the United States and the West for not only economic assistance, but also political and military support.

Conclusion

Discussion of how the Iran-Iraq war will end and how the governments of the day in Baghdad, Tehran, Moscow, and Washington will behave toward one another at that time is, of course, highly speculative, especially as the war seems likely to continue. As long as the war continues, Iraq will work hard to remain friends with the USSR in order to receive Soviet military assistance. At the same time, Iraq will continue to pursue a friendly policy toward the United States and the West not only to expand its economic relations with them, but also to keep them from undertaking actions that benefit Iran. Once the war is over, an independent government in Baghdad may well move to further friendly relations with the United States and the West for aid and investment to restore Iraq's economy—a task for which the USSR is much less helpful. Still, Iraq would be likely to continue to rely on the USSR for military assistance, though its overall need may diminish after the war is over. Iraq might also seek more to diversify its arms suppliers because of the Soviet arms cutoff at the beginning of the war as well as to reduce dependence on one supplier in any future conflict. An Iraq dominated by Iran would have to follow Iran's lead—a situation both superpowers have an interest in preventing because Moscow would stand to lose an ally in Iraq while U.S. friends in the GCC would also be threatened.

Whether or not the war is prolonged, it is clear that an independent government in Baghdad derives benefits from friendship with both superpowers that it would like to see continue. Similarly, it has important disagreements with both that will limit how closely Baghdad will ally itself with either. In political terms, Baghdad has had differences with Moscow over the Horn of Africa, Afghanistan, and the Iraqi Communist Party, but these have not prevented Soviet-Iraqi cooperation. The one political issue that could harm these ties is if Soviet-Iranian relations improve markedly. With the United States,

Iraq has had differences over the Arab-Israeli conflict, but the restoration of diplomatic relations shows that Iraq is prepared to downplay these differences somewhat. Whether this continues to be true after the war ends remains to be seen.

A U.S.-Iranian rapprochement is one political issue that the Iraqis do not have to worry about at present. With regard to bilateral relations, Iraq is concerned over U.S. criticism of Iraqi use of chemical weapons and the possibility of the U.S. Congress demanding Baghdad be put back on the list of countries that support terrorism. The Iraqis worry that such moves could signal the end of the U.S. predisposition toward Iraq and a relaxation of U.S. concern that its allies cease exporting arms to Iran. Iraq would like to remain on friendly terms with both superpowers, but to whatever extent either one pursues policies harmful to Iraqi interests, Baghdad is likely to rely more heavily on the other.

Notes

1. On Iraq's internal politics, see Christine Moss Helms, *Iraq: Eastern Flank of the Arab World* (Washington, D.C.: Brookings, 1984).

2. For the history of Soviet relations with Iraq and Iran, see Aryeh Y. Yodfat, *The Soviet Union and the Arabian Peninsula* (London: Croom Helm; New York: St. Martin's Press, 1983).

3. There were, however, some East European arms deliveries to Iraq during this period. From 1958 up until the outbreak of the war, the USSR had delivered over $7 billion worth of arms to Iraq but less than $1 billion worth to Iran. According to the International Institute for Strategic Studies, the USSR made several large arms sales to Iraq in 1979, including MiG-23/-25/-27 fighters, Mi-8 helicopters, and large numbers of self-propelled howitzers. In October 1980, just after the war began, the IISS reported that Moscow sold and delivered 145 T-62 medium tanks to Iraq. The next Soviet arms sale to Iraq it reported occurred in January 1983, was worth about $2 billion, and included fighter aircraft, tanks, surface-to-surface missiles (SSMs), and surface-to-air missiles (SAMs). Since then, the Soviets have sent unspecified quantities of tanks, SSMs, and probably other weapons.

See U.S. Central Intelligence Agency, *Communist Aid Activities in Non-Communist Less Developed Countries, 1979 and 1954–79* ER 80-103187 (October 1980), pp. 29–30; Stephen T. Hosmer and Thomas W. Wolfe, *Soviet Policy and Practice toward Third World Conflicts* (Lexington, Mass.: Lexington/D. C. Heath, 1983), p. 74; U.S. Arms Control and Disarmament Agency, *World Military Expenditures and Arms Transfers, 1971–1980* (March 1983), p. 119; *The Military Balance 1980–1981* (London: IISS, 1980), p. 103; *The Military Balance 1981-1982*, p. 115; *1983–1984*, p. 129; and *1984–1985*, p. 143.

4. William B. Quandt, *Saudi Arabia in the 1980s: Foreign Policy, Security, and Oil* (Washington, D.C.: Brookings Institution, 1981), p. 21.

5. See Zalmay Khalizad, "Islamic Iran: Soviet Dilemma," *Problems of Communism* 33:1 (January-February 1984), pp. 15–16.

6. On U.S.-Iraqi relations, see Frederick W. Axelgard, *U.S.-Arab Relations: The Iraq Dimension*, National Council on U.S.-Arab Relations Occasional Paper Series: No. 5 (1985).

7. On the recent improvement in Soviet-Iranian relations, see Albert L. Weeks, "Experts on Soviets See a Clear Tilt Toward Iran," *New York City Tribune*, April 30, 1985, p. 1, and Albert L. Weeks, "Host of Soviet Advisers Reported in Iran," *New York City Tribune*, May 1, 1985, p. 1.

8. Iraq had begun purchasing arms from the West, especially France, before the war began and has continued to do so since then. Nevertheless, Iraq still relies mainly on Soviet weapons. For example, by mid-1984, Iraq had acquired some 5 Super Etendards and 49 Mirages from France, but out of a total inventory of about 580 combat aircraft, 500 of them were from the Soviet Union. For an estimate of Iraq's current weapons inventory, see *The Military Balance 1984–1985* (London: IISS, 1984) pp. 62–63.

9. Soviet economic aid commitments to Iraq totaled $705 million for the entire period 1959–1979. No further aid commitments were made by Moscow to Baghdad from 1980 through 1983; figures for subsequent years are unavailable. By contrast, the United States has extended Iraq over $1.8 billion in agricultural credits since December 1982 alone. See CIA, *Communist Aid, 1979*, p. 29; Department of State, *Soviet and East European Aid*, p. 19; U.K. Foreign Ministry, *Soviet East European and Western Development Aid 1976–1983* (Foreign Policy Document No. 108), p. 25; and Axelgard, *U.S.-Arab Relations* pp. 20–21.

Selected Bibliography

Abdulghani, J. M. *Iraq and Iran: The Years of Crisis*. London and Sydney, Australia: Croom Helm, 1984.

Al Eyd, Khadim A. *Oil Revenues and Accelerated Growth: Absorptive Capacity in Iraq*. New York: Praeger, 1979.

American Embassy Baghdad. *Foreign Economic Trends and their Implications for the United States: Iraq*. Washington, D.C.: U.S. Department of Commerce, various years.

Axelgard, Frederick W. "The Tanker War in the Gulf." *Middle East Insight* 3, no. 6 (November/December 1984): 26–33.

————. *U.S-Arab Relations: The Iraq Dimension*. National Council on U.S.-Arab Relations Occasional Paper Series: no. 5, 1985.

Batatu, Hanna. *The Old Social Classes and the Revolutionary Movement of Iraq: A Study of Iraq's Old Landed and Commercial Classes and of its Communists, Ba'thists, and Free Officers*. Princeton, N.J.: Princeton University Press, 1978.

Cordesman, Anthony H. "The Gulf Crisis and Strategic Interests: A Military Analysis." *American-Arab Affairs* 9 (Summer 1984): 8–15.

————. *The Gulf and the Search for Strategic Stability*. Boulder, Colo.: Westview Press, 1984.

Dawisha, Adeed I. "Iraq: The West's Opportunity." *Foreign Policy* 41 (Winter 1980-81): 134–153.

Devlin, John. *The Ba'th Party*. Stanford, California: Hoover Institution Press, 1976.

Economist Intelligence Unit Ltd. "Iraq: A New Market in a Region of Turmoil." *Economist Intelligence Unit Special Report 88* (October 1980).

Farid, Abdel Majid, ed. *Oil and Security in the Arabian Gulf*. Papers presented at an international symposium sponsored by the Arab Research Centre in 1980. New York: St. Martin's Press, 1981.

Fukuyama, Frances. *The Soviet Union and Iraq since 1968*. Santa Monica, Calif.: The Rand Corporation, 1980.

Ghareeb, Edmund. "The Forgotten War." *American-Arab Affairs* 5 (Summer 1983): 59–75.

————. "Iraq: Emergent Gulf Power." In *The Security of the Persian Gulf*, edited by Hossein Amirsadeghi. London: Croom Helm, 1981.

————. "Iraq and Gulf Security." In *The Impact of Iranian Events upon U.S. and Persian Gulf Security*, A. Michael Szaz, project director. Washington, D.C.: American Foreign Policy Institute, 1979.

_____. *The Kurdish Question in Iraq.* Syracuse, N.Y.: Syracuse University Press, 1981.

al-Hasani, Abd al-Razzaq. *Tarikh al-Wazarat al-Iraqiyya* (History of the Iraqi Governments), vol. 3 (same title). Beirut: Dar al-Kuttub Press, 1974.

Helms, Christine Moss. *Iraq: Eastern Flank of the Arab World.* Washington, D.C.: The Brookings Institution, 1984.

_____. "The Iraqi Dilemma: Political Objectives versus Military Strategy." *American-Arab Affairs* 5 (Summer 1983): 76–85.

Hosmer, Stephen T., and Wolfe, Thomas W. *Soviet Policy and Practice toward Third World Conflicts.* Lexington, Mass.: Lexington/D.C. Heath, 1983.

Hussein, Saddam. *Al-Turath al-Arabi wal Mu'asara (Arab Heritage and Contemporary Life).* Baghdad: Dar al-Huriya. 1978.

Iskander, Amir. *Saddam Hussein.* Paris: Hatchette, 1980.

Ismail, Tareq Y. *Iraq and Iran: Roots of Conflict.* Syracuse, N.Y.: Syracuse University Press, 1982.

Jabir, Kamil Abu. *Arab Ba'th Socialist Party.* Syracuse, N.Y.: Syracuse University Press, 1966.

Jawdat, Nameer Ali. "Reflections on the Gulf War." *American-Arab Affairs* 5 (Summer 1983): 86–98.

Kelidar, Abbas. *The Integration of Modern Iraq.* New York: St. Martin's Press, 1979.

_____. "Iraq: The Search for Stability." *Conflict Studies* 59 (July 1975): 1–21.

Khadduri, Majid. *Arab Contemporaries.* Baltimore: Johns Hopkins University Press, 1973.

_____. *Independent Iraq,* 2nd ed. London: Oxford University Press, 1966.

_____. *Political Trends in the Arab World.* Baltimore: Johns Hopkins University Press, 1972.

_____. *Republican Iraq, A Study on Iraqi Politics since the Revolution of 1958.* London: Oxford University Press, 1969.

_____. *Socialist Iraq, A Study in Iraqi Politics since 1968.* Washington, D.C.: Middle East Institute, 1978.

McLachlan, Keith, and Joffé, George. "The Gulf War: A Survey of Political Issues and Economic Consequences." *The Economist Intelligence Unit Special Report 176.* London: The Economist Publications Ltd, 1984.

al-Najjar, Mustafa. *Al-Tarikh al-Siyassi li-Alaqat al-Iraq al-Dawliyya bil-Khalij.* Basra: Basra University Press, 1975.

Neumann, Robert G., and Hunter, Shireen T. "Crisis in the Gulf: Reasons for Concern but Not Panic." *American-Arab Affairs* 9 (Summer 1984): 16–21.

Niblock, Tim, ed. *Iraq: The Contemporary State,* London and Canberra, Australia: Croom Helm, 1982.

Nyrop, Richard F., ed. *Iraq, A Country Study.* Washington, D.C.: Foreign Area Studies, American University, 1979.

Penrose, Edith Tilton. *Iraq: International Relations and National Development.* Boulder, Colo.: Westview Press, 1978.

Quandt, William B. "The Gulf War: Policy Options and Regional Implications." *American-Arab Affairs* 9 (Summer 1984): 1–7.

Stiven, William. *Supremacy and Oil: Iraq, Turkey, and the Anglo-American World Order.* Ithaca, N.Y.: Cornell University Press, 1982.

Tahir-Kheli, Shirin, and Ayubi, Shaheen, eds. *The Iran-Iraq War: New Weapons, Old Conflicts.* New York: Praeger, 1983.

United Kingdom Foreign Ministry, *Soviet, East European, and Western Development Aid 1976–1983.* Foreign Policy Document no. 108 (n.d.).

Wright, Claudia. "Iraq-New Power in the Middle East." *Foreign Affairs* 58, 2 (Winter 1979/80) 257–277.

About the Editor and Authors

Frederick W. Axelgard is a fellow in Middle East Studies at the Center for Strategic and International Studies (CSIS) with research interests in the stability of the Persian Gulf, U.S. Middle East policy, and the Iran-Iraq war. He holds degrees from Brigham Young University and the Fletcher School of Law and Diplomacy, Tufts University. He is also Washington correspondent for the London-based magazine, *Middle East International*. His articles have appeared in several major U.S. newspapers and journals, including the *Los Angeles Times, American-Arab Affairs, Defense & Foreign Affairs*, and the *Christian Science Monitor*.

Adeed Dawisha is presently a fellow at the Woodrow Wilson Center for International Scholars at the Smithsonian. Born in Iraq, Dawisha studied at Lancaster University and the London School of Economics. He has been deputy director of studies at the Royal Institute of International Affairs in London and a visiting professor at the School of Advanced International Studies of Johns Hopkins University. His books include *Egypt in the Arab World* (New York: Wiley, 1976), *Syria and the Lebanese Crisis* (New York: St. Martin's Press, 1980), and *Islam in Foreign Policy* (Cambridge, England: Cambridge University Press, 1983).

Jonathan Crusoe is a writer for the *Middle East Economic Digest (MEED)*. Since 1979, he has covered Iraq for *MEED*, providing principal support as well for their research on Kuwait and North and South Yemen. Born in Kuwait and educated in England, he took his degree in English and Arabic at Leeds University.

Edmund Ghareeb holds a doctoral degree in history from Georgetown University and is a consultant in Washington for Middle Eastern and media affairs. He has served as correspondent for a number of Arab, American, and European publications. His published works include *The Kurdish Question in Iraq* (Syracuse, N.Y.: Syracuse University Press, 1981), "Iraq: Emergent Power in the Gulf" in Hossein Amirsadeghi, ed., *The Security of the Persian Gulf* (New York: St. Martin's Press, 1981), and *Split Vision: The Portrayal of Arabs in the American Media* (Washington, D.C.: American Arab Affairs Council, 1983).

Mark N. Katz is research associate at the Kennan Institute for Advanced Russian Studies and has been a visiting scholar at CSIS. He is currently finishing a book entitled *Russia and Arabia: Soviet Foreign Policy toward the Arabian Peninsula* (Baltimore: Johns Hopkins University Press, 1986). His doctoral thesis at the Massachusetts Institute of Technology was published as *The Third World in Soviet Military Thought* (Baltimore: Johns Hopkins University Press, 1982).

Index

46   119